THE TWENTY-FIRST CENTURY
UNIVERSITY

Faculty
Development
Program
JH109

BUTLER
UNIVERSITY

omplicated

A Book Series of Curriculum Studies

William F. Pinar
General Editor

VOLUME 32

PETER LANG
New York • Washington, D.C./Baltimore • Bern
Frankfurt am Main • Berlin • Brussels • Vienna • Oxford

Lisa K. Childress

THE TWENTY-FIRST CENTURY
UNIVERSITY

Developing Faculty Engagement
in Internationalization

PETER LANG
New York • Washington, D.C./Baltimore • Bern
Frankfurt am Main • Berlin • Brussels • Vienna • Oxford

Library of Congress Cataloging-in-Publication Data

Childress, Lisa K.
The twenty-first century university: developing faculty engagement
in internationalization / Lisa K. Childress.
p. cm. — (Complicated conversation; v. 32)
Includes bibliographical references and index.
1. International education. 2. Multicultural education. 3. Education, Higher—
Research. 4. Universities and colleges—Faculty. I. Title.
LC1090.C533   378'.016—dc22   2009014917
ISBN 978-1-4331-0659-0
ISSN 1534-2816

Bibliographic information published by **Die Deutsche Nationalbibliothek.**
Die Deutsche Nationalbibliothek lists this publication in the "Deutsche
Nationalbibliografie"; detailed bibliographic data is available
on the Internet at http://dnb.d-nb.de/.

The paper in this book meets the guidelines for permanence and durability
of the Committee on Production Guidelines for Book Longevity
of the Council of Library Resources.

Printed in the United States of America

This book is dedicated to
my husband, Trey, and my son, Jacob,
who continue to inspire me every day.

Table of Contents

Figures

Tables

Acknowledgments

Completing a book, just like operationalizing an internationalization plan, requires a team of ardent supporters. Fortunately, I could not have asked for a stronger team of advocates and champions. Collectively, my team gave me the push, pull, and perspective I needed to complete this manuscript.

To my book series editor, William Pinar: I thank you for your belief in the importance of faculty engagement in internationalization and encouragement of the publication of this manuscript.

To my mentors, Sharon McDade, Christa Olson, and Jim Williams: The interest you have taken in my scholarship has been fundamental in seeing this manuscript through to fruition. I am honored that such esteemed higher education, internationalization, and international education experts have taken the time to challenge me to extract the fundamental principles embedded in my findings, and for pushing me to articulate them with authority.

To Susan Buck Sutton and Barbara Hill: I am very grateful that as such accomplished internationalization experts, you have taken the time to share your insights to strengthen my research and writing.

To Madeleine Green: I will forever be grateful that you opened the door to my foray in internationalization research. I have learned a great deal from your scholarship and leadership in the field.

To Uliana Gabara, Gilbert Merkx, and all of the University of Richmond and Duke University faculty and administrators who shared their time and insights with me: This study would not have been possible without your participation. I thank you for taking the time to share your stories with me and for your thoughtfulness about how faculty have engaged in internationalization at your institutions. Uliana and Gil, I have learned a tremendous amount from your leadership of Richmond and Duke's internationalization and from your leadership in the field at large.

To my parents-in-law, Joan and Don: Thank you for your unconditional support and love, which helped to fuel this project through to completion.

To my brothers and sisters-in-law, Jay, Jordan, Matthew, Gianina, Marcie, and Sarah: Your belief, interest, and pride in my success have meant the world to me. You have helped me to keep my sense of humor and have encouraged me more than you know.

To my dad: Thank you for encouraging me to focus on "Mission Possible." You always helped me to see the connections between my findings and the big picture.

To my mom: Your unwavering belief in my abilities has fueled my ambitions and has given me much strength to overcome the hurdles to see this manuscript through to completion. Thank you also for taking care of Jacob, so I could focus on the book!

To my husband and best friend, Trey: I could not ask for a more committed partner in everything I do. Your daily display of love, your incredible sense of humor, and your phenomenal cooking gave me the sustenance to focus and persevere with this important project.

To my son, Jacob, who was born when the contract for this manuscript arrived in the mail: Thank you for inspiring me to be the best person I possibly can be. Your smiles and love make all the hard work worthwhile.

Chapter I

Introduction

Historical Context of Internationalization

Internationalization has become an increasingly important trend in higher education. Recent national and global events, such as September 11th and the War on Terror have demonstrated the importance of international knowledge for national security and global peace. Rapidly changing demographics in local, regional, and international communities have underscored the importance of cross-cultural understanding and communication in order to enable individuals to effectively contribute across an array of professions. As noted by Thomas Friedman (2000, 2005) in *The Lexus and the Olive Tree: Understanding Globalization* and *The World Is Flat: A Brief History of the Twenty-first Century*, constant technological advances, such as the Internet, have broken down cultural and national barriers that previously existed in commerce, such that businesses seek individuals who have knowledge of business practices and cultures around the world, as well as the skills necessary to communicate across borders. Collectively, these changes require the development of knowledge and skills necessary to adapt and lead in a world with expanding intercultural interactions and decreasing monocultural dimensions. Higher education institutions serve critical roles in this process as they develop knowledge systems, and contemporary knowledge systems are increasingly international.

This is not a new development for higher education. During the latter half of the twentieth century, major world events served as catalysts for universities and colleges to focus on international education. Higher education leaders turned their attention to the importance of international education after World War II when "the American Council on Education, the President's Commission on Higher Education, the philanthropic foundations, and the [US] Congress joined forces to counteract the exclusively Western orientation of the curriculum" (Rudolph, 1977, p. 264). At governmental levels, this reorientation was implemented by the Fulbright Act of 1946 and the National Defense Education Act (NDEA) of 1958. In particular, in the wake of World War II, the Fulbright Act established an exchange scholarship system for students and educators between the US and other countries. In response to Sputnik, the NDEA supported universities in investing in teaching and research on international and foreign area studies. As such, World War II and

Sputnik provided an impetus for an increased focus on international education.

Accordingly, numerous national organizations conducted studies and issued reports to alert higher education administrators and faculty of the urgent need to internationalize their institutions. For instance, shortly after the passage of the NDEA, at the request of the US Department of State, the Ford Foundation, a major private source of support for higher education institutions' international initiatives, developed a committee of university, foundation, business, and government leaders to systematically analyze and clarify the international role of universities and suggest ways that higher education institutions could perform more effectively in world affairs. This committee issued a report entitled "The University and World Affairs," which emphasized the responsibility of university faculty to educate students about world affairs, despite the "largely sporadic and unplanned" attempts in existence (Committee on the University and World Affairs, 1960, p. 2). The report called for the transcendence from the traditionally domestic and Western orientation of scholarship and training to the integration of international dimensions into undergraduate, graduate, and professional curricula. As faculty are central to such integrative initiatives, the importance of faculty involvement in internationalization emerged from the Committee on the University and World Affairs' report.

Echoing this call for the internationalization of higher education institutions, in 1965, Education and World Affairs, a nonprofit organization created to study and assist in strengthening the international teaching, research, and service dimensions of colleges and universities, advocated the importance of both institutional and individual approaches to promoting international education. First, Education and World Affairs asserted that a strategic, intentional, institution-wide approach was critical in order to integrate an international dimension into a higher education institution in a meaningful way. Second, in addition to this institutional approach, an individual approach was recommended in order to strategically reach out to individual faculty, disciplines, and colleges to encourage their engagement in international education. As such, Education and World Affair's report highlighted the importance of a strategic internationalization plan that accounts for overarching institutional priorities, as well as specific departmental and faculty needs.

Two decades later, the American Association of State Colleges and Universities (AASCU) conducted a study in which the AASCU vice president for international programs, Maurice Harari, surveyed AASCU institutional members about their internationalization efforts. Based on analysis of the data collected from 77.19% of the AASCU membership (264 institutions), Harari (1981) concluded that "the degree of internationalization of a campus is not a function of size, location, or overall budget. In the last analysis it is a function of faculty competence and commitment and of institutional leadership" (p. 29). Harari advanced this point in his 1989 report to answer "What does it take to internationalize an institution?" (p. 3). In response to this question, Harari (1989) emphasized

> There is no substitute to a consensus-building process which must be initiated and nurtured on campus. It is this process which ideally will yield the true commitment of the faculty and the administration. A statement of commitment which is not the result of a careful faculty-administration institution consensus-building process is easily perceived . . .as no more than public relations verbiage. (p. 3)

Harari's (1981, 1989) reports underscored that in order to implement the strategic internationalization plan advocated by Education and World Affairs, an intentional process to engage faculty is critical.

The need to develop faculty engagement in internationalization was also affirmed by the Association of American Colleges (1985), which asserted that it is faculty who ultimately have the authority to foster students' international education, as they control the curriculum. Thus, faculty should be encouraged to consider whether their curricula are designed to advance students' understanding of foreign nations and cultures. Yet, the report acknowledged that although calls for international education had become prevalent, such intentional, systematic efforts to develop faculty support remained rare. Although no specific reason for why strategies to engage faculty to participate in international education initiatives was stated, the Association of American Colleges (1985) did note the existence of "obstacles to faculty responsibility that are embedded in academic practice" (p. 9). This report confirmed that despite the importance and challenges of developing faculty engagement in internationalization, little is known empirically about strategies to advance such faculty involvement.

Lambert (1989) emphasized both the importance and challenge of faculty engagement in internationalization in his comprehensive review of international studies at the undergraduate level, which was conducted on behalf of the American Council on Education. He concluded that although faculty involvement is key to advancing students' international knowledge, "institutions...cannot and should not attempt to micromanage the content of individual international studies course—this is rightly the preserve of individual faculty members and departments" (p. 167). In order to advance students' international understanding, Lambert (1989) found that "cross-course, cross-departmental, cross-school, cross-function innovation and coordination" (p.

148) was necessary. Yet, the question of how to develop such faculty engagement and coordination remained unanswered.

To address these challenges and offer pragmatic recommendations, in the following decade, the Association of International Education Administrators (1995) issued guidelines for internationalizing higher education institutions, which were addressed directly to administrators and faculty and included the following: (a) develop an international education goal statement; (b) build links among disciplines and colleges; (c) reform the core curriculum to integrate an international perspective into the content, cultures, and disciplines addressed; and (d) include international activities in faculty reward policies. In order to achieve these objectives, AIEA (1995) confirmed the findings of other higher education associations that institution-wide faculty participation and communication are essential.

In response to these calls, many institutional leaders have expressed intentions for internationalization. As such, Green and Schoenberg (2006) noted that "it would be difficult to find a college or university today that is not making some effort to internationalize" (p. 1). Yet, a gap remains between the rhetoric for and implementation of internationalization (Siaya & Hayward, 2003). Even as recently as 2006, higher education association leaders have noted that institutional leaders' rhetoric is insufficient for realizing an institution's internationalization goals. As voiced by Marlene Johnson, CEO and executive director of NAFSA: Association of International Educators (NAFSA), "High-level rhetoric about the value of educational exchanges, while encouraging, is not a substitute for policy" (NAFSA: Association of International Educators, 2006b, para. 4). Thus, despite consistent calls for internationalization over the past half century, implementation remains challenging, and therefore lacking, in many higher education institutions.

Key Problems Facing University Administrators and Faculty

In response to these recommendations and challenges, increasing numbers of colleges and universities have created internationalization plans and campus-wide committees in order to develop the widespread faculty engagement necessary to advance the institution's internationalization goals. In particular, internationalization plans—written commitments to internationalization—have emerged as organizational tools through which institutions seek to inform and stimulate faculty participation in international initiatives. Yet, internationalization scholars and practitioners alike have indicated that a significant gap exists between the development of plans and the development of institution-wide faculty involvement necessary to implement the stated goals (Altbach, 2002; Engberg & Green, 2002; Knight, 1994; Olson, Green, & Hill, 2005; Schoorman, 1999; Wood, 1990). Although internationalization plans serve the important function of articulating an institution's goals, Engberg and Green (2002) noted that "the challenge is to create an institutional culture in which internationalization is lived rather than merely spoken about" (p. 15). Thus, in order to affect an institution's culture, it is not only important that institutions develop concrete plans for internationalization, but that they operationalize those plans.

To address this challenge, many institutions have developed campus-wide committees as organizational mechanisms through which to facilitate the collective leadership necessary to implement their internationalization plans. This is evidenced by studies conducted by the American Association of State Universities and Colleges (1981) and American Council on Education (Green, 2005), which found, respectively, that 73.7% and 86% of institutions highly active in internationalization have a campus-wide committee dedicated to overseeing and carrying out internationalization initiatives. Hence, campus-wide committees increasingly serve as the organizational subunits that senior administrative leaders charge with the responsibility of operationalizing institutions' internationalization goals.

Although these committees are usually comprised of a small group of committed internationalists (Thullen et al., 2002), the engagement of a critical mass of faculty throughout the institution, spanning many disciplines, is required in order for internationalization plans to becoming living documents on campus and affect the institutional ethos. Extensive faculty involvement is critical because internationalization, a process of institutional transformation, "cannot be owned by a small group, as it then becomes marginalized and can be seen as an exclusive, rather than inclusive, issue" (Knight, 1994, p. 12). Thus, the operationalization of internationalization plans is dependent upon the widespread engagement of faculty.

There is evidence, however, that faculty outside of the campus-wide internationalization committee are often unaware of the committee, its directives, and initiatives (Ellingboe, 1998). In addition to this lack of awareness, institutional and individual barriers exist, which hinder faculty engagement in international activities. Consequently, the lack of awareness of faculty at large of institutions' internationalization plans and committees creates significant challenges for committees to develop a critical mass of faculty supporters in order to implement institutions' internationalization plans. Although evidence is strong that it is important for campus-wide committees to communicate the vision and goals of the internationalization plan to faculty throughout the institution (e.g., Aigner et al., 1992; Liverpool, 1995;

Viers, 2003), a gap remains in understanding how those goals are communicated so that widespread faculty participation is stimulated. The problem facing internationalization leaders addressed by this study was that despite the rhetoric in higher education for internationalization, significant barriers exist in developing faculty engagement in internationalization.

Theoretical Framework

From a theoretical perspective, Knight's (1994) internationalization cycle framed this investigation. This framework indicates that institutions proceed through six interconnected phases of internationalization, which include (a) awareness, (b) commitment, (c) planning, (d) operationalization, (e) review, and (f) reinforcement (see Figure 1). Yet, how can campus leaders transition from the planning phase to the operationalization phase of internationalization? This study addressed this question by using Knight's internationalization cycle as a framework through which to investigate the strategies used at two higher education institutions to engage faculty in the operationalization of internationalization plans.

Specifically, Knight's framework indicates that a critical mass of faculty supporters is a prerequisite for success in both the planning phase and the subsequent operationalization phases. This model posits that organizational practices (such as those employed by campus-wide committees) and organizational principles (such as those reflected in internationalization plans) directly impact faculty involvement in internationalization. Thus, Knight's model provided a useful lens through which to understand how the academic activities, organizational practices, and organizational principles employed at two institutions affected faculty engagement in the operationalization of internationalization plans.

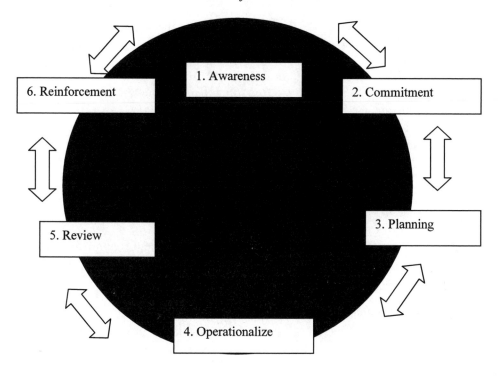

1. Awareness

6. Reinforcement

2. Commitment

5. Review

3. Planning

4. Operationalize

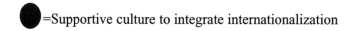 =Supportive culture to integrate internationalization

Figure 1. Internationalization cycle. From "Internationalization: Elements and Checkpoints," by J. Knight, 1994, Canadian Bureau for International Education Research, 7, p. 12. Copyright 1994 by Jane Knight and Canadian Bureau for International Education. Reprinted by permission of the publisher. All rights reserved.

Definition of Key Terms

This section contains conceptual definitions used in this book.

Internationalization is the process of integrating an international and intercultural dimension into the teaching, research, and service functions of a higher education institution (Knight, 1994, 1999, 2004).

Comprehensive internationalization is "a strategic and integrated approach to internationalization in which institutions articulate internationalization as an institutional goal (if not priority), develop an internationalization plan driven by sound analysis, and seek to bring together the usually disparate and often marginalized aspects of internationalization" (Olson et al., 2006, p. vi).

An internationalization cycle is a sequence of six phases through which a higher education institution proceeds in order to integrate an international dimension into institutional systems and values (Knight, 1994). This study focused on the transition from the planning to operationalization stages, which was a previously unexamined area of research.

An internationalization plan is defined as higher education institutions' written commitments to internationalization, including goals, mission statements, vision statements, implementation plans, allocated resources, or timelines.

Operationalization is the process of "implementing the different aspects of a strategy and creating a supportive culture" (Knight, 1994, p. 13). This term is used interchangeably with implementation.

An internationalization committee is an ongoing group that is (a) comprised of faculty and administrators who represent a wide range of departments and (b) charged by a senior institutional leader with the authority and resources to coordinate or oversee an institution's internationalization.

An internationalization taskforce is a short-term group that is (a) comprised of faculty and administrators who represent a wide range of departments and (b) charged by a senior institutional leader with a specific, time-limited task, e.g., the development of an internationalization plan.

Developing faculty engagement is the process of stimulating faculty interest and involvement in a particular initiative. This term is used interchangeably with developing faculty participation and involvement.

Chapter II

Critical Analysis of the
Internationalization Literature

Internationalization has become a frequently espoused term in higher education. It has been defined in a multitude of ways and has been studied across a host of disciplines from business to engineering to higher education. In business, internationalization has been defined as the process of adapting business' operations, including strategy, structure, and resources, to international environments (Calof & Beamish, 1995). In engineering, internationalization has been defined as the modification or design of software so that it can be understood and used in different languages, countries, or cultures (Lionbridge, 2006; Sun Developer Network, 2006). In higher education, internationalization has been defined in multiple ways, which has contributed to confusion about its meaning and purpose.

Although some higher education leaders have conceptualized internationalization as a series of individual, international components, others have interpreted internationalization as a holistic, integrative process. For example, NAFSA (2003) explained internationalization as a collection of international activities, including study abroad by US students, study in the US by international students, faculty exchanges, foreign language training, international development projects, corporate and university partnerships, and campus community interactions. Yet, others have conceptualized internationalization as the process of integrating an international perspective into the curriculum, in particular (Groennings & Wiley, 1990, Harari, 1989, 1992; R. Lambert, 1989; Mestenhauser, 1998; Tonkin & Edwards, 1981).

Still, others have conceptualized internationalization as an integrative process that involves not only the curriculum, but all institutional activities (Engberg & Green, 2002; Green & Olson, 2003; Green & Shoenberg, 2006; Harari, 1981; Knight, 1994; Olson et al., 2005). In particular, Knight (1994, 1999, 2004) defined internationalization as the process of integrating an international and intercultural dimension into the teaching, research, and service functions of a higher education institution. By conceptualizing internationalization as a process rather than as a series of individual components, this definition situates internationalization as a continual effort of infusing international and intercultural perspectives into an institution's curricular and co-curricular policies, programs, and activities (Knight, 1994; Olson, 2005). The advantage of Knight's (1994, 1999, 2004) definition is that it situates internationalization as a system-wide, holistic process. As such, it lays the foundation for understanding the importance of developing widespread faculty participation in order to affect an institution's tripartite mission of teaching, research, and service.

Whereas Knight (1994) provided a useful general process definition of internationalization, the American Council on Education (ACE) has developed a more thorough and practical definition of comprehensive internationalization. ACE has defined comprehensive internationalization as "a strategic and integrated approach to internationalization in which institutions articulate internationalization as an institutional goal (if not priority), develop an internationalization plan driven by sound analysis, and seek to bring together the usually disparate and often marginalized aspects of internationalization" (Olson et al., 2006, p. vi). In particular, ACE has emphasized that comprehensive internationalization is both broad and deep and, thereby, leads to institutional transformation (Engberg & Green, 2002; Green & Olson, 2003; Green & Shoenberg, 2006; Olson et al., 2005, 2006). Specifically, for comprehensive internationalization to infiltrate a campus, international perspectives must be (a) broadly integrated into departments, administrative units, curricula, and co-curricular programs and (b) deeply expressed in institutional culture, values, policies, and practices (Olson et al., 2005).

This book employs Knight's (1994, 1999, 2004) definition of internationalization to frame the examination of strategies that affected faculty engagement in the integration of an international dimension into their institutions' teaching, research, and service. This book also draws upon ACE's definition of comprehensive internationalization (Engberg & Green, 2002; Green, 2003c; Green & Shoenberg, 2006; Olson et al., 2005, 2006) to assess how these strategies inspired faculty in all corners of the university to integrate international perspectives into their own scholarship and, thereby, advance the implementation of their institutions' internationalization plans.

Rationales for Internationalization

It is critical to understand what motivates institutions to integrate an international dimension into their teaching, research, and service. Examination of these motivations is important as the rationales are multiple and "different rationales imply different means and ends to internationalization" (de Wit, 2002, p. 84). Knight's (1999) categorization of the rationales into academic, economic, political, and social-cultural groupings provides a useful framework for understanding institutional motivations for internationalization.

Economic Rationales

Economic rationales are prominent for the internationalization of higher education institutions. The literature is replete with studies that indicate that internationalization is important to prepare students for domestic and international careers, to generate income for the institution, and to contribute to economic development and competitiveness (Brecht & Walton, 2001; Collins & Davidson, 2002; de Wit, 2002; Goodwin & Nacht, 1988; Government Accountability Office, 2007; Green, 2003c; Gutek, 1993; James & Nef, 2002; Knight, 1999, 2004; Lim, 1996, 2003; Mallea, 1977; E. L. Miller, 1992; Moxon, O'Shea, Brown, & Escher, 2001; National Association of State Universities and Land Grant Colleges Task Force on International Education, 2004; Organisation for Economic Co-operation and Development, 1995; Scott, 1992; Steers & Ungsen, 1992; Viers, 1998). In the 1980s and 1990s, the economic motivation for internationalization derived from corporations' drive for economic competitiveness in the global market (Green, 2003). With the subsequent infiltration of the Internet into business and civic life, this technological revolution has blurred the boundaries between foreign and domestic concerns. Consequently, "globalization has reached a point where the United States cannot expect to retain its competitive edge if its workforce lacks strong international and cross-cultural skills and knowledge" (Alliance for International Educational and Cultural Exchange & NAFSA: Association of International Educators, 2006, p. 1). Therefore, as the Committee for Economic Development (2006), an independent, nonpartisan policy and research organization, asserted, businesses are in need of employees with the knowledge and skills to interact effectively with diverse cultures, so that businesses can address the complexities of global competition and prosper in an increasingly international environment (E. L. Miller, 1992; Steers & Ungsen, 1992). In addition to business leaders, higher education leaders often view internationalization in terms of its economic benefits. Many institutions have indicated, based on economic rationales, that the primary component of their internationalization strategy is the recruitment of international students (Hayward, 2000). Because international students generally do not receive financial support from colleges and universities (Institute for International Education, 2005, 2006c), institutional leaders often regard international students as an important source of enrollment and revenue for their institutions. On a national level, international students contribute more than $13 billion to the US economy, including significant contributions to US higher education institutions (Institute for International Education, 2005, 2006). Thus, there are strong economic rationales for higher education leaders to internationalize their institutions through the recruitment of international students.

Moreover, it is not only business and education leaders who have been driving the economic demand for internationalization of higher education; individual citizens have also indicated that they believe global knowledge and skills are keys to economic success. As indicated in ACE's survey of 1,000 individuals over the age of 18 on their attitudes about international education, more than 50% of respondents thought that knowledge of events outside the US would be important to their careers in 10 years and 90% thought that it will be important to the careers of future generations (Siaya & Hayward, 2001). In particular, this study highlighted a specific skill that 86% of respondents believed will assist them in obtaining a job—foreign language competency. These findings were echoed in NAFSA's (2006a) survey of a broad cross-section of 1,000 adults, in which 92% of respondents agreed that knowledge of other languages will give future generations a competitive advantage in career opportunities. Collectively, these two national studies are illustrative of individual citizens' concurrence with business and higher education leaders that an international education is important for economic competitiveness and success.

Political Rationales

Given significant world events of the past century, political rationales for the internationalization of colleges and universities have become major motivating forces for political and higher education leaders, as well as individual citizens. In the twentieth century, World Wars I and II and the Cold War increased individuals' interest in international education (Aigner, Nelson, & Stimpfl, 1992; Hayward, 2000). In response to the recognition that knowledge of the world outside US borders is necessary to develop foreign policy and ensure national security (Green, 2003a), during the Cold War, international affairs research, particularly studies focused on peace and security issues, became a major funding area for government agencies and foundations (Hayward, 2000). The goal of these funding agencies was largely to promote area and foreign language studies as well as study abroad programs to create expertise in the interest of minimizing national threats (Alliance for International Educational and Cultural Exchange & NAFSA: Association of International Educators, 2006).

Although many individuals and institutions turned inward after the Cold War (Alliance for International Educational and Cultural Exchange & NAFSA: Association of International Educators, 2006), the attack on the World Trade Center on September 11, 2001, underscored the continuing political importance of international education. As a response to September 11, the internationalization of higher education institutions has gained prominence as a means through which to equip students with an awareness of world cultures and skills necessary to address national security and foreign policy (Alliance for International Educational and Cultural Exchange & NAFSA: Association of International Educators, 2006; Green, 2003c; National Association of State Universities and Land Grant Colleges Task Force on International Education, 2004). Thus, political rationales for internationalizing universities and colleges have been prominent over the past century and have gained increased momentum after September 11.

Academic Rationales

The internationalization of higher education is important academically, as it is a means to strengthen liberal education and enhance the quality of teaching and research (de Wit, 2002; Green, 2003c; Knight, 1999; Lim, 2003; Reichard, 1983). Internationalization, in fact is an intrinsic component of the academic mission of universities as the concept of universe is embedded in the concept of university (Knight, 1999). Thus, the academic interest in internationalization at many institutions has translated into a desire to develop students' global critical thinking skills. In order to provide opportunities for students to develop these skills, higher education leaders have called for the internationalization of curriculum (Bond, 2003; Bremer & van der Wende, 1995; Burn, 1980; Cogan, 1998; Engberg & Green, 2002; Freedman, 1998; Green & Shoenberg, 2006; Groennings & Wiley, 1990; Harari, 1989, 1992; National Association of State Universities and Land Grant Colleges Task Force on International Education, 2004; Odgers & Giroux, 2006; Shute, 2002), increased presence and integration of international students on university campuses (Alliance for International Educational and Cultural Exchange & NAFSA: Association of International Educators, 2006; NAFSA: Association of International Educators, 2006b; Reichard, 1983), and increased support for study abroad programs (Commission on the Abraham Lincoln Study Abroad Fellowship Program, 2005). In particular, through these academic initiatives, students (a) gain a knowledgeable and diversified worldview, (b) comprehend international dimensions of their major fields of study, (c) communicate effectively in another language and/or cross-culturally, and (d) exhibit cross-cultural sensitivity and adaptability (National Association of State Universities and Land Grant Colleges Task Force on International Education, 2004).

These academic rationales for internationalizing colleges and universities have been echoed by individual citizens. In a survey conducted by the American Council on Education (Siaya & Hayward, 2001) on individuals' attitudes on international education, 86% of respondents expressed that the presence of international students enriches the learning experience of university students. This finding was further supported by NAFSA's (2006a) survey of individuals' attitudes on international education, in which, respectively, 94%, 86%, and 77% of respondents expressed that learning about global cultures, interacting with international students, studying abroad are important components of education. As evidenced, academic rationales serve as important driving forces for the internationalization of universities and colleges, in order to develop student's global awareness and critical thinking.

Socio-cultural Rationales

Social and cultural motivating forces for internationalization include the desire to increase students' abilities to live an increasingly multicultural environment and to contribute to international understanding (Aigner et al., 1992; Brecht & Walton, 2001; de Wit, 2002; Goodwin & Nacht, 1988; Green, 2003c; James & Nef, 2002; Lim, 2003; McKellin, 1998; Merkx, 2003; Reichard, 1983). In particular, internationalization of higher education has been lauded as a critical means through which to develop students' intercultural communication skills, which are necessary to address the increasing cultural and ethnic diversity within and between countries (de Wit, 2002; Deardorff, 2006; Knight, 1999). Moreover, through a commitment to internationalization, institutions can support faculty research and consulting to aid developing countries (Green, 2003b; Reichard, 1983; Smuckler, 2003). In this researcher's extensive review of the scholarly and practitioner literature on internationalization, social and cultural rationales emerged as the least frequently cited motivating forces for internationalizing higher education institutions. Perhaps the relative lack of focus on these rationales is due to their intangible benefits. For instance, as the attainment of intercultural competence is difficult to measure (Deardorff, 2006), especially when compared to academic knowledge, which is measured through higher education examinations; economic success, which is measured through employment status and compensation; and political knowledge, which is measured by government employment examinations. Yet, it is clear that some higher education institutions employ social and cultural rationales for internationalization, in order to enhance students and faculty's cross-cultural knowledge and skills necessary to contribute to international development.

Summary

In summary, there are four overarching rationales for the internationalization of higher education institutions: economic, political, academic, and socio-cultural. An understanding of these rationales lays the foundation for why institutions may develop internationalization plans and why faculty may engage in the operationalization of those plans. These rationales shed light on the importance of considering the diverse motivating factors at work as internationalization plans are implemented. A combination of these rationales (and counter arguments to these rationales) are likely present on a given campus. It is helpful for internationalization leaders to be aware of the full range of rationales when working to engage a broad swath of the institution in an internationalization initiative.

Recommendations from Internationalization Leaders

Internationalization practitioners and scholars have recognized that institutional commitments, communication channels, and widespread faculty engagement are critical to internationalization. This section will address these recommendations from internationalization leaders.

First, an explicit, intentional plan is critical to guide and legitimize institutional stakeholders' involvement in international activities (Aigner et al., 1992; Harari, 1989; Knight, 1993; Leinwald, 1983; Mestenhauser, 2002; Moats-Gallagher, 2004; National Association of State Universities and Land Grant Colleges, 1993; National Association of State Universities and Land Grant Colleges Task Force on International Education, 2004; Olson et al., 2005, 2006; Scott, 1992). It is through these written commitments to internationalization that departments and faculty can develop an understanding of how and why to integrate international dimensions into their work.

Second, communication channels are critical to convey institutional goals, policies, and practices that support internationalization (Harari, 1981; Knight, 1993; Olson et al., 2005; Thullen et al., 2002). Through communication channels such as campus-wide committees, departments and faculty can share resources and information on international teaching, research, and service in order to maximize institutional resources and impact (Aigner et al., 1992; Bowman, 1990; Green & Olson, 2003; Harari, 1981, 1989; Mestenhauser, 2002; National Association of State Universities and Land Grant Colleges Task Force on International Education, 2004; Thullen et al., 2002).

Finally, widespread faculty participation is essential for an institution to realize its goals for internationalization (Bond, 2003; Chandler, 1999; Cleveland-Jones, Emes, & Ellard, 2001; Green & Olson, 2003; Harari, 1981; National Association of State Universities and Land Grant Colleges, 1993; National Association of State Universities and Land Grant Colleges Task Force on International Education, 2004; Olson et al., 2005; Thullen et al., 2002; Welsh, 1997). As faculty have authority over the focus of their curricula, research, and service, the development of a critical mass of faculty supporters throughout an institution enables an international dimension to be infused into an institution's ethos and activities.

Internationalization Plans

Internationalization scholars and practitioners alike have found that an institution's development of an internationalization plan—a written commitment to internationalization—is indispensable to the realization of an institution's internationalization goals (e.g., Aigner et al., 1992; Ellingboe, 1998; Francis, 1993; Green & Olson, 2003; Knight, 2004; Knight & de Wit, 1995; Lim, 1996; McKellin, 1995; National Association of State Universities and Land Grant Colleges, 1993; Olson et al., 2006; Paige, 2005). This is so because internationalization "requires articulating explicit goals and developing coherent and mutually reinforcing strategies to reach them" (Engberg & Green, 2002, p. 10).

Roles of Internationalization Plans

Institutions' written commitments for internationalization serve three overarching roles: articulating institutional commitment, providing a road map, and serving as a tool to develop buy-in. First, internationalization plans serve the important function of articulating an institution's commitment to infusing an international perspective throughout the campus. As institutional subunits often model their own priorities and activities to support institutional goals, a written commitment to internationalization highlights the importance of international education to the institution and its stakeholders.

Second, an internationalization plan can serve as a road map for internationalization. Considering the diversity of internal and external stakeholders in internationalization, an internationalization plan can help to provide a coherent direction for institutional priorities. By delineating practical steps, institutional stakeholders are able to understand how they can participate (Knight, 1994). Thus, a written articulation of an institutions goals and intended direction for internationalization can address the finding in numerous studies that a lack of understanding of what internationalization means impedes institutions' attainment of its goals for internationalization.

Finally, an internationalization plan can serve as a tool to develop buy-in. By explicitly articulating institutional rationales and goals for infusing the campus with an international perspective, internationalization plans can stimulate the involvement and support of internal stakeholders, such as faculty, administrators, and students, as well as external stakeholders, such as alumni, foundations, government agencies, and higher education institutions overseas. Particularly on a financial level, a written commitment and goal statement helps institutions to demonstrate to internal and external funding sources, including alumni, foundations, government agencies, international not for profit agencies, that their institution is serious about internationalization. Thus, by explaining and clarifying institutional goals for internationalization, written plans serve as a tool to develop the buy-in from key stakeholders, whose support is critical to transition an institution from the planning to operationalization stages of internationalization.

Recommendations from Internationalization Leaders

Internationalization plans should contain four major components: (a) goals, (b) allocated resources, (c) action items, and (d) timelines and targets. First, the internationalization plan should include a statement of the international education goals for the institution, including desired global competencies for students (Knight, 1994; Moats-Gallagher, 2004; Olson et al., 2006; Paige, 2005). It is useful for the internationalization plan to allocate financial and human resources, necessary for the implementation of the stated goals (Olson et al., 2006; Paige, 2005; Siaya & Hayward, 2003). For instance, financial resources may include budgets for academic exchanges, faculty development workshops, international curricular development grants, and grants received or sought after for international research activities. Human resources may include necessary faculty involvement in international research, teaching, and service, as well as administrators whose responsibility it is to manage international academic exchanges, curricular development workshops, and research grants. Thus, it is important for internationalization plans to build on existing institutional strengths, resources, and faculty expertise.

Moreover, a delineation of specific action items that support and implement the institution's internationalization goals is important to translating the internationalization plan from rhetoric into action (Olson et al., 2006; Paige, 2005). In particular, an internationalization plan should explain different initiatives through which faculty can participate in the implementation of the institution's internationalization goals. This is important as the broader the base of faculty involvement, the more widely an internationalization plan will be implemented. As such, it is important for organizational mechanisms to be developed to promote communication and sharing information of international activities among institutional units.

Finally, timelines and targets for accomplishing specific objectives serve the important function of providing the structure necessary to advance the institutional agenda (Knight, 2001; Knight & de Wit, 1995; Moats-Gallagher, 2004; Olson et al., 2005, 2006; Paige, 2005). An institution's internationalization goals need to be put into practical and achievable steps, as this sense of movement and accomplishment generates support. In order for this support to evolve, it is similarly important that internationalization goals are made transparent to internal and external stakeholders.

Further, it is important for an institution to allow its internationalization goals to evolve from year to year and to make them transparent to internal and external stakeholders. In sum, through the inclusion of goals, inputs, activities, timelines, and targets internationalization plans provide the road map necessary to legitimize, stimulate, and direct stakeholder involvement, so that the goals can be implemented.

Insights from Strategic Planning Scholarship

Although internationalization scholars have documented the roles and components of internationalization plans, little has been written about the implementation of internationalization plans. Therefore, it is useful to consult the strategic planning literature for valuable insights into factors that can support the implementation of internationalization plans. Upon analysis of this body of scholarship, the author synthesized these factors into the "Five I's of Strategic Plan Implementation": (a) intentionality, (b) information, (c) involvement, (d) institutional networks, and (e) incentives.

Intentionality. Intentionality is at the core of a strategic plan's development and implementation (e.g., Bolinger, 1990; Canary, 1992; Dooris, Kelley, & Trainer, 2002; Keller, 1999; Kezar, 2005; Liedtka, 1998; Peterson, 1999; Rowley, Lujan, & Dolence, 1997). As such, a strategic plan must be developed consciously and purposefully to achieve the desired goals in light of an institution's particular context (Keller, 1999; Peterson, 1999). In particular, consideration of how a strategic plan interfaces with an institution's governance, administrative, leadership, and information-sharing patterns is critical, as a strategic plan is neither an isolated document nor is its implementation an isolated process (Canary, 1992; Keller, 1999). Therefore, it is essential that planning leaders explicitly consider a strategic plan's impact upon and relationship with institutional subunits. Accordingly, strategic planning leaders schould proactively encourage subunit leaders to define their own ways to implement the strategic plan within their units (Keller, 1999; Kezar, 2005; Peterson, 1999). Such intentional alignment with institutional subunits enables a strategic plan to directly address unique subunit priorities and foster a sense of shared ownership of the strategic plan throughout the institution.

Information. Sharing information related to the strategic plan throughout an institution is essential to a strategic plan's implementation (Bean & Kuh,

1984; Canary, 1992; Dill & Helm, 1988; Kanter, 1994; Keller, 1999; Lerner, 1999; Peterson, 1999; Rowley et al., 1997). This is particularly important as strategic planning scholar Marvin Peterson (1999) noted, "Quite often, initiatives that reflect a new institutional role, mission, or mode of doing business are not readily perceived" (p. 69). Considering that a strategic plan is likely to fail if constituents lack knowledge about it, strategic planning experts assert that institutional leaders should widely disseminate information about a strategic plan's rationales, components, resources, as well as opportunities and incentives for involvement (Armstrong & Brown, 2006; Bean & Kuh, 1984; Dill & Helm, 1988; Kanter, 1994; Peterson, 1999). Moreover, information about successful efforts in implementing a strategic plan should be shared and reinforced through both (a) internal means of communication, such as internal reports, newsletters, and seminars, and (b) external means of communication, such as external newspapers and other media, and reports in professional journals (Peterson, 1999; Rowley et al., 1997). Overall, communication of information both inside and outside an institution is critical to the continued development of awareness, support, and implementation of a strategic plan.

Involvement. Implementation of a strategic plan requires widespread involvement of an institution's constituents (Armstrong & Brown, 2006; Bean & Kuh, 1984; Bolinger, 1990; Canary, 1992; Dill & Helm, 1988; Lawler, 1992; Lerner, 1999; Peterson, 1999; Rowley et al., 1997). This is so, as widespread involvement—the engagement of participants throughout an institution—increases the diversity of ideas and creates a sense of shared ownership in a strategic plan, which ensures continued implementation of the plan. Yet, barriers to involvement are significant and include factors such as constituent workload, specific skills and knowledge necessary for participation, and institutional policies and practices (Peterson, 1999). To overcome these barriers and increase involvement in a strategic plan, three action steps should be considered. First, special training may be necessary to develop essential skills and knowledge bases necessary to facilitate constituent participation. Second, existing institutional policies may need to be reviewed and potentially revised in light of a strategic plan's goals. Third, it is essential that the opportunities for involvement are well publicized and easily accessible. Through such practices, it is possible to ensure that the implementation of a strategic plan does not become the province of a few, but instead becomes the shared responsibility of all institutional constituents.

Institutional networks. Institutional networks are critical to fostering the collaboration and resources necessary to implement a strategic plan (Armstrong & Brown, 2006; Bean & Kuh, 1984; Bolinger, 1990; Kezar, 2005;

Lerner, 1999; Rowley et al., 1997). An institutional network is a coalition, alliance, or complex set of relationships among a group of constituents that is useful in accomplishing a present or future goal (Kezar, 2005). Leveraging these networks is especially important in order to realize institution-wide goals for which collaboration among disparate stakeholders is required.

In particular, institutional networks serve two overarching functions in the implementation of a strategic plan. First, institutional networks provide vehicles for ideas, such as (a) implementation initiatives and (b) types of necessary financial resources, human resources, and incentives to flow and gain momentum. Second, institutional networks provide the intellectual and social resources needed to overcome resistance to new institutional goals and processes. To maximize the potential for institutional networks to facilitate the implementation of a strategic plan, it is important to create "feedback loops" (Birnbaum, 1988, p. 183) to intentionally connect, educate, and involve institutional stakeholders in the implementation of a strategic plan through activities such as faculty, administrator, and student orientation programs, leadership symposia, and social events (Kezar, 2005). Such intentional networking forums cultivate the involvement of change agents, provide opportunities for new constituents to participate, and connect constituents who might develop new networks to advance the goals and implementation of a strategic plan.

Incentives. Incentives are undoubtedly the key to developing participation in a strategic plan (Armstrong & Brown, 2006; Bean & Kuh, 1984; Lerner, 1999; Peterson, 1999). Organizational learning and human behavior research indicates that individuals participate in activities for which they get rewarded (Armstrong & Brown, 2006; Brown, 2001; Herzberg, 2003; Lerner, 1999). Thus, in order for strategic plans to succeed, constituents should be rewarded for their participation in activities that advance the plan's goals. Provision of incentives at both the subunit and individual levels are critical to developing widespread participation in the strategic plan (Armstrong & Brown, 2006; Bean & Kuh, 1984; Lerner, 1999; Peterson, 1999). Such incentives to encourage involvement can take the form of rewards or recognition. Rewards can include financial and human resources support, release time from other duties, and other forms of developmental assistance. Recognition can include the incorporation of strategic planning goals into an institution's evaluation, promotion, and hiring guidelines, as well as the development of an award to recognize outstanding involvement in advancing a strategic plan. Therefore, in order to stimulate the participation of a critical mass of constituents in the implementation of a strategic plan, it is critical to provide rewards and recognition at both the professional and psychological levels.

Summary. The strategic planning scholarship is instructive for understanding factors that can facilitate the implementation of internationalization plans. First, it is critical that internationalization plan leaders intentionally consider how the plan connects with the institution's administrative, leadership, and information-sharing systems. As such, strategic planning scholars suggest that it is useful for planning leaders to consider the plan's impact upon institutional subunits and encourage subunit leaders to define their own implementation initiatives for the internationalization plan goals. Second, in order to implement an internationalization plan, it is important to develop a plan for wide and continued dissemination of information related to the plan's rationales, components, and resources. Third, planning leaders should proactively adapt programs and policies to facilitate widespread involvement in internationalization, such as through special training programs and policy revisions. Fourth, internationalization plan advocates should employ institutional networks to develop implementation initiatives and build support for internationalization throughout the campus. Finally, it is critical that planning leaders provide incentives to implement internationalization plan goals through rewards and recognition in the institution's evaluation, promotion, and hiring guidelines. Thus, by applying the "Five I's of Strategic Plan Implementation"—intentionality, information, involvement, institutional networks, and incentives—internationalization plan leaders can facilitate the implementation of their institutions' goals for internationalization.

Campus-wide Internationalization Committees

Campus-wide internationalization committees, also known as internationalization teams or international education committees, are prevalent organizational mechanisms through which institutions can integrate international activities into their ethos, policies, and practices. Organizational mechanisms, in general, are critical for internationalization, as they provide a structure necessary to facilitate the development and communication of international initiatives to maximize their effect throughout the institution. Campus-wide internationalization committees, in particular, are important organizational mechanisms frequently employed by senior institutional leaders, such as presidents, provosts, and vice provosts for international affairs, who give a group of faculty and administrators from a wide range of departments a particular charge relating to internationalization. This charge may include developing, coordinating, or overseeing the implementation of institutional goals for internationalization. As Biddle (2002) noted, "Over the last

15 years, large numbers of university faculty and administrators have spent a great many hours on task forces, working groups, and committees charged with designing plans to 'internationalize' or 'globalize' their institutions" (p. 5). In particular, studies conducted by the ACE (Green, 2005) and the American Association of State Colleges and Universities (AASCU) (Harari, 1981) found that campus-wide committees are frequently employed by higher education institutions seeking to implement their internationalization goals. Specifically, in ACE's study (Green, 2005), 86% of research universities surveyed reported the presence of an internationalization committee on their campuses. In AASCU's (1981) study, 73.7% of member institutions that were found to have high levels of internationalization reported the presence of internationalization committees. Thus, many higher education institutions are seeking to implement their internationalization goals through the use of campus-wide committees.

These committees are particularly important, as integrating an international dimension throughout a campus cannot be achieved through the work of a single person, department, or a written plan. Rather, through the coalition of constituent units, each bringing their strengths, ideas, and concerns for implementation, an institution's internationalization goals can be realized. Moats-Gallagher (2004) emphasized this point by asserting "In an era where global concerns require interdisciplinary approaches, the coordination of campus international programs across academic units is vital" (p. 2). Because faculty are key participants in institutional change, it is important for a diverse group of faculty to take ownership of the development and implementation of an institution's internationalization plans.

Roles of Campus-wide Internationalization Committees

Campus-wide committees serve three overarching roles: to build bridges, foster collective leadership, and provide an organizational structure. These three roles are detailed in the following sections.

Build bridges. Comprehensive internationalization requires the development of connections across academic units. In order to foster interdisciplinary connections, campus-wide internationalization committees bring together diverse academic representatives to discuss and share new initiatives, existing programs, and priorities for internationalization (National Association of State Universities and Land Grant Colleges Task Force on International Education, 2004; Olson et al., 2006). By bringing together faculty from a wide array of disciplines, campus-wide committees enable faculty to learn about the various international teaching, research, and service projects occurring throughout the campus, which may serve as springboards to interdisciplinary collaborations in order to address particular international issues (Knight, 1994). As such, campus-wide committees build bridges among internationalization stakeholders who would not otherwise be communicating or collaborating on campus activities.

In particular, campus-wide committees create formal and informal communication channels. These communication channels are particularly important as internationalization information and initiatives are often dispersed throughout a campus. Moreover, these communication channels address a prevalent internationalization conundrum: in efforts to internationalize, institutions often end up with a disconnected collection of international activities.

Through the communication channels opened through campus-wide committees, departments and faculty are enabled to share information, leverage existing institutional resources, and develop partnerships to advance individual, departmental, and institutional goals related to internationalization. Campus-wide committees are particularly important in building bridges across faculty and departments: "Because internationalization activities can easily become isolated and fragmented, information-sharing through both formal and informal channels is important to make better use of resources, promote collaboration where appropriate, and ensure that opportunities are made available to the widest possible segment of the population" (Knight, 1994, p. 8). Thus, through the communication channels opened by regular campus-wide committee meetings, faculty from diverse disciplines are enabled to understand how their individual or departmental initiatives could reinforce or complement one another. Through this sharing of information and resources, faculty from various departments can form coalitions and alliances, which provide political advantages for developing the foundation for campus-wide participation and buy-in necessary to carry out internationalization plans. As such, campus-wide committees build bridges to harness the human, technical, and financial resources required to implement an institution's internationalization plan.

Foster collective leadership. Due to the complexity of internationalization as a process of institutional transformation, collective leadership for internationalization is essential. Consequently, the process of individually initiating and implementing reform is impractical, if widespread institutional impact is intended. As such, campus-wide committees serve the critical function of fostering collective leadership for internationalization. This is particularly important, as "the strength [of internationalization] lies in the whole being greater than the sum of its parts, especially for impact, benefit, and leverage" (Knight, 1994, p. 5). As campus-wide committees bring together a team of individuals who presumably believe in and understand the importance of international education to their disciplines and to the institution, in the words of the National Association of State Universities and Land-Grant Colleges (NASULGC) Task Force on International Education (2004), campus-wide internationalization committees create the "bench strength for change" as they form a "coalition of the converted" (p. 39). This collective leadership is particularly important in operationalizing an internationalization plan, as research has indicated that in order to institutionalize an initiative, inter-departmental cooperation and the empowerment of stakeholders is imperative.

Provide organizational structure. Campus-wide committees provide an organizational structure critical for the development of an institution's commitment, planning, implementation or monitoring of internationalization, depending upon the group's charge. As internationalization calls for intentional and systematic implementation, campus-wide committees can provide a clearinghouse for international activities taking place throughout the institution. The importance of an organizational structure is supported by Harari (1989), who noted "Irrespective of the size, location or resources of a campus, it is clear that the institution needs to have a locus of responsibility and leadership for its international activities" (p. 6). In addition, campus-wide committees serve as an evident, tangible symbol of an institution's commitment to internationalization. If internal and external institutional stakeholders have questions or ideas about the institution's internationalization, the campus-wide committee serves as the organizational unit that stakeholders can approach.

This organizational structure is particularly important for three reasons. First, since there are many diverse stakeholders working to help an institution to respond and adapt to an increasingly diverse, globally focused environment, campus-wide committees provide an organizational structure for coordinating these stakeholder interests and initiatives. Second, as Knight (1994) pointed out: "Even if there are an increasing number of academic activities taking place, if they are not underpinned by a permanent organizational commitment and structure, they may die when proponents leave the institution" (p. 5). Third, with the diversity of stakeholder interests and initiatives, campus-wide committees "provide a structure for building consensus" (Thullen, 2002, p. 29). Thus, through the organizational structure they provide, campus-wide committees are enabled to take a "macro perspective of what is happening across the institution and how different aspects could reinforce or complement activities" (Knight, 1994, p. 13).

Furthermore, campus-wide committees bring together a diverse group of stakeholders from across the campus, which provides a forum for illuminating how an institution's internationalization agenda aligns with and can reinforce other institutional initiatives. Such an awareness of alignment with other institutional initiatives can serve to not only further the implementation of internationalization plan goals, but advance other institutional objectives, as well. In summary, campus-wide committees are important for internationalization as they build bridges, foster collective leadership, and provide organizational structure. As comprehensive internationalization both broadly and deeply affects an institution, campus-wide committees are important to fostering the interdisciplinary coordination and cooperation necessary for the operationalization of institutional plans for internationalization.

Recommendations from Internationalization Leaders

Internationalization experts concur on four recommendations for committee composition and activities that have the potential to advance the operationalization of internationalization plans. First, campus-wide internationalization committees should be composed of faculty who are (a) highly respected, (b) committed to integrating an international dimension into their disciplines and institution at large, and (c) represent diverse academic departments (Back et al., 1996; Backman, 1984; Harari, 1981; Olson et al., 2006). In addition, ACE suggested that senior institutional administrators and administrators specializing in international education services are important members of the committee (Olson et al., 2006). As for the committee chairperson, Backman (1984) advised that this position is held by a faculty member who is "highly respected by both colleagues and administrators—one that is knowledgeable, and yet not narrow-minded, with a strong sense of responsibility and the requisite management skills to meet a timetable, allow for adequate input, and still achieve consensus" (p. 342). These recommendations account for the significant challenges involved in developing faculty involvement in institutional initiatives, particularly in regards to internationalization.

Second, it is useful for committees to inventory faculty to assess their internationalization interests, areas of expertise, as well as general disciplinary strengths and weaknesses relating to internationalization (Backman, 1984; Harari, 1981; Thullen et al., 2002). In particular, ACE has recommended that universities and colleges can build a strategic framework for internationalization by conducting a thorough internationalization review process (Green & Olson, 2003; Olson et al., 2005). As advocated by the American Association of State Colleges and Universities (Harari, 1981), "Systematically taking stock of views, resources, and potential is essential to the consensus-building process necessary to identify and implement the international needs of the institution" (p. 29). Third, by holding open forums to invite faculty suggestions and feedback on international initiatives, campus-wide committees can structure opportunities for faculty engagement in an institution's internationalization plan (Backman, 1984; Childress, 2009; Thullen et al., 2002). Finally, as a means to increase understanding of how to communicate the internationalization plan goals across diverse campus stakeholders, it may be useful to invite external consultants to meet with campus-wide committees and non-committee faculty members (Childress, 2009; Thullen et al., 2002).

Chapter III

Faculty Engagement in Internationalization

Successful internationalization efforts are dependent upon faculty engagement. Several factors account for this contention. To begin with, faculty have long been recognized as key forces in institutional transformation and the internationalization of knowledge. This is understandable, as faculty directly impact the teaching, research, and service missions of higher education institutions. In particular, faculty have direct involvement and authority in (a) curricular content changes, (b) research, scholarly collaboration, and interdisciplinary engagement, and (c) international development and service. Given this authority, faculty have the ability to decide whether or not to incorporate international perspectives into their curricula, draft grant proposals for international research, or participate in international development projects. Therefore, as faculty are stewards of an institution's teaching, research, and service agendas, research indicates that widespread faculty engagement in internationalization is not optional, but essential for an entire campus to be affected.

Faculty Role in the Internationalization of the Curriculum

In particular, faculty are pivotal in the internationalization of the curriculum. As internationalization of curricula involves (a) infusing Western and non-Western perspectives into courses and (b) offering students opportunities to compare and contrast issues across cultural perspectives, it is faculty who have the authority to direct students' international learning. This means that faculty can choose to model the knowledge, behaviors and values of an "international mind-set" (Paige, 2003, p. 58) or a parochial, ethnocentric point of view. Thus, faculty attitudes toward the value of international perspectives in the curriculum greatly impacts students' learning.

Internationalization of the curriculum is especially important, given the changing demographics of students attending US higher education institutions (Olson et al., 2005, 2006). Although many higher education institutions have traditionally relied upon study abroad programs as a means through which to develop students' international mind-set, with the increasing numbers of adult, part-time, and working students who have multiple commitments and responsibilities, fewer students may choose to participate in study abroad programs (Green, 2002). In particular, a recent ACE study indicated that only 10% of college students study abroad (Siaya & Hayward, 2003). With the current trend in college student demographics, this number is likely to decrease. Therefore, it is more important than ever that faculty engage in internationalizing the curricula, as through that process the majority of students will be enabled to develop an international mind-set.

In order to internationalize their curricula, faculty need specific knowledge, skills, and attitudes, as well as institutional support. In terms of knowledge, faculty need an awareness of their discipline's literature as it relates to other cultures and societies and a clear understanding of the objectives for internationalizing their courses. In terms of personal attitude, faculty need a desire and willingness to change their courses. As for institutional support, faculty need (a) adequate time to prepare course modifications, including release time during the academic year or time off during the summer, (b) sufficient resource materials in libraries, and (c) travel funds to conduct research abroad. Collectively, these requirements for faculty involvement in internationalization suggest that widespread faculty support of internationalization is not endogenous. Therefore, faculty engagement in internationalization must be proactively encouraged and supported by campus leaders overseeing the implementation of internationalization plans.

Levels of Faculty Engagement

There are various levels of faculty engagement in internationalization (Carter, 1992; Deutsch, 1970; Goodwin & Nacht, 1983; Green & Olson, 2003; Morris, 1996). These levels include champions, advocates, latent champions and advocates, uninterested, skeptics, and opponents. Champions are faculty with vast knowledge of international issues in their areas of expertise and strong cross-cultural communication skills. As such, these faculty are likely to be committed to participating in the implementation of their institution's internationalization plans. Advocates are faculty who are passionate about a particular aspect of internationalization. This enthusiasm for internationalization is often buttressed by a faculty member's international experiences and foreign language proficiencies. Thus, advocates are faculty to whom campus-wide committees and other internationalization leaders can call upon for support in order to operationalize particular components of an internationalization plan.

Latent champions and advocates may exist on campus. Although at present these faculty members' eyes may glaze over when internationalization is mentioned, through exposure to international issues connected to their scholarly and personal interests, such as through teaching and research opportunities overseas or through hearing about the value of international educational exchanges through family and friends, these potential supporters may discover the value of internationalizing their teaching and research with strategic support. In other words, if latent supporters are invited into the process and provided with the right experience and incentives, they could be transitioned from latency into advocacy for internationalization (Green & Olson, 2003).

Skeptics are those who are doubtful of the relevance of international issues to their disciplines. Thus, they are often hesitant to participate in their institution's internationalization plans. Finally, opponents are faculty who openly disagree with and make efforts to obstruct the implementation of internationalization plans. The rationales behind such skepticism and opposition may vary, but may include a belief of national superiority, lack of international experience, or fear of losing status or resources (Green & Olson, 2003).

Challenges in Developing Faculty Engagement in Internationalization

Despite the importance of faculty engagement to successful internationalization efforts, numerous obstacles exist which impede faculty involvement in internationalization. As faculty are, in general, known to be resistant to change, it should come as no surprise that there is considerable faculty resistance to internationalization, which is inherently a change process. In particular, some faculty do not recognize the benefits of infusing international perspectives in their teaching, research, and service. Bond (2003) described this lack of motivation as "faculty intransigence" (p. 8), which obstructs the implementation of institutions' internationalization goals. Yet, a degree of faculty resistance to internationalization may in fact be constructive in ensuring that the internationalization plan and its implementation strategies address faculty and departmental needs.

In order to develop widespread faculty involvement, the engagement of latent supporters, skeptics, and opponents is critical. Green and Shoenberg (2006) emphasized that generating the involvement of faculty whose support may be dormant is both essential and challenging to the implementation of an institution's internationalization goals:

> Experience with many important education initiatives has shown that it is comparatively easy to get the enthusiastic agreement of a small group of committed people to lay out a particular course of action and generate ideas for its implementation.

The problem is generating sufficient interest and action from the thousands of faculty members on the front lines to make the recommendations a reality. (p. 22)

Given this juxtaposition of the importance and challenges of developing faculty engagement in internationalization, it is important to understand the sources of resistance to internationalization.

Specifically, the challenges of engaging faculty in internationalization have been characterized by leading internationalization scholars (Bond, 2003; Green & Olson, 2003) as institutional and individual barriers. This categorization serves as a useful lens through which to synthesize the challenges in developing widespread faculty engagement in internationalization.

Institutional Barriers

Institutional barriers can significantly impede faculty engagement in internationalization. To highlight the connection between institutional infrastructure and faculty engagement in internationalization, the National Association of State Colleges and Universities (1993) asserted that "faculty can only play an active role [in internationalization] if an environment is created that ensures that professional development, scholarship, and public service in the international setting are valued" (p. 6). Yet, three specific types of institutional barriers obstruct faculty engagement in internationalization, including lack of financial resources, disciplinary divisions and priorities, and restrictive tenure and promotion policies (Green & Olson, 2003).

Lack of financial resources. Lack of financial resources prevents the development of incentives for faculty to engage in international activities. Engberg and Green (2002) noted that "the most frequently cited reason for inaction in higher education is lack of funding" (p. 16). Internationalization is no exception to this tendency. Financial constraints preclude faculty from participating in teaching, research, and consulting projects overseas for meaningful periods of time (Ellingboe, 1998), due to the significant costs embedded in traveling and working overseas, as well as filling teaching vacancies on the home campus precipitated by a faculty member's work overseas. Therefore, without financial support, faculty lack the resources necessary to promote their involvement in international teaching, research, and service activities.

Prevalent rationales for the lack of financial resources for internationalization include the increase of financial constraints placed upon institutions combined with their increasing expectations, which makes internationalization "yet another undervalued, unfunded initiative" (Bond, 2003, p. 9). In addition, Ellingboe (1998) emphasized that some senior institutional administrators perceive "faculty development [as the] responsibility of individual faculty and their departments, and will consequently not allocate any central funds to internationalize the faculty" (p. 211). Hence, due to increasing institutional financial cutbacks combined with dissension about the locus of responsibility for faculty development, lack of financial resources likely constrains the development of widespread faculty engagement in the operationalization of internationalization plans.

Disciplinary divisions and priorities. Academic disciplines—the organizational subsystems for faculty scholarship—can limit faculty participation in international activities. There are four overarching reasons why disciplinary orientations serve as barriers to faculty engagement in internationalization. First, the disciplinary focus impacts faculty members' exposure to and training in integrating international perspectives in their fields. Although some disciplines are "intrinsically international, global, or comparative in nature" (Green & Shoenberg, 2006, p. 5), knowledge bases in other disciplines are largely constructed from a domestic point of view. In concurrence, Maidstone (1996) pointed out that "Faculty typically understand their discipline or field, and teach it in the way they themselves were taught. Transformations of consciousness do not, therefore, come about easily" (p. 37). Thus, faculty members' participation in internationalization efforts is largely dependent upon the international focus, or lack thereof, of their disciplines, as this disciplinary focus directly impacts faculty members' academic training in the international issues in their fields.

Second, faculty tend to prioritize their teaching and research agenda based on the current needs and issues of their disciplines rather than their institutions. This prioritization can impede their involvement in institutional initiatives, such as the implementation of an institution-wide internationalization plan. Hence, if department chairs and disciplinary associations do not emphasize the importance of international issues to their disciplines, faculty may lack motivation to focus on international teaching, research, and service projects, as these activities may not advance their publication and tenure opportunities.

Third, divisions between disciplines can preclude the interdisciplinary collaboration that is increasingly important in order to realize internationalization plan goals. Ellingboe (1998) affirmed this point as she acknowledged "disciplinary walls are often high, hard to scale, and difficult to tear down to create bridges across disciplines in interdisciplinary courses, programs, team-teaching, and faculty collaboration" (p. 212). In other words, the decentralized, "each tub on its own bottom" (Altbach, 2006, p. 49) approach to academic organization precludes the inter-departmental communication that is necessary to share international teaching and research resources across the institution. Therefore, these inter-departmental barriers prevent the across-department communication and collaboration that is necessary for internationalization to reach its fullest potential, as internationalization as a holistic process is predicated on communication across disciplines in order to ensure that international perspectives become infused into the institutional ethos.

Finally, not only does the lack of interdisciplinary partnerships and communication hinder faculty from participating in internationalization to their fullest potential, but the politics involved in developing consensus for internationalization within departments is often complex and difficult. Specifically, intra-departmental politics can obstruct the development of consensus and action on a department's internationalization agenda. Therefore, both intradisciplinary and interdisciplinary barriers preclude the development of faculty engagement that is essential to fulfill an institution's internationalization plan goals.

Restrictive tenure and promotion policies. Many higher education institutions do not explicitly include international teaching, research, and service in their tenure and promotion policies. In general, the faculty reward system in contemporary higher education does not acknowledge the advantages and usefulness of faculty international experiences to advancing institutional goals for internationalization Siaya and Hayward (2003) confirmed this contention in their national surveys, which examined the extent of institutional commitment to internationalization. In their surveys, Siaya and Hayward (2003) found that only 4% of US colleges and universities included international scholarship and service in their tenure and promotion policy policies. Consequently, faculty participation in internationalization activities, such as integrating international perspectives into courses, applying for grants to conduct international research, and applying for fellowships to teach overseas, tend not to be recognized and rewarded in tenure and promotion policies. As such, these restrictive tenure and promotion policies create a lack of incentives for faculty to engage in internationalization efforts.

But specifically why and how does the focus of tenure and promotion policies on the domestic milieu hinder faculty engagement in internationalization? In the National Association of State Universities and Land Grant College's (NASULGC's) (1993) examination of the barriers to faculty participation in internationalization, the authors concluded that as a result of the majority of tenure and promotion criteria omitting international components, "faculty perceive international engagements as jeopardizing to their careers" (p. 3). Thus, the development of widespread faculty engagement in internationalization is at odds with prevailing academic reward structures. Even though some faculty will neither infuse international perspectives into their courses nor participate in research, teaching, or service overseas without incentives to do so, research indicates that institutional policies at many institutions fail to reward faculty engagement in internationalization.

Individual Barriers

Three major types of individual barriers to faculty engagement in internationalization exist, which include faculty attitudes toward international learning, personal knowledge and skills, and cognitive competence (Ellingboe, 1998; Green & Olson, 2003).

Attitudes toward international learning. Faculty members' attitudes toward international learning directly impact their willingness and interest to internationalize their courses, engage in research collaboration with international partners, and participate in service projects overseas. Although champions and advocates of internationalization tend to demonstrate positive attitudes toward the value of international perspectives for their work, skeptics and opponents tend to view international learning as extraneous to their personal and professional goals, including their academic objectives for their students (Green & Olson, 2003).

Based upon research to date, faculty who do not value international learning are less inclined to participate in international education opportunities, as such involvement may "challenge their perceptions of the world and their place in it" (Green & Olson, 2003, p. 73). Faculty skeptics and opponents of internationalization prefer to focus on the domestic milieu to advance students' intellectual and social development. Further, the negative attitude of some faculty toward internationalization can result from their concern that an institution's focus on an internationalized curriculum is symbolic of a shift toward a consumer-oriented approach toward higher education, which diverts attention away from the core knowledge valued within a traditional curriculum. As such, these faculty may view the infusion of international perspectives into their course content or pedagogy as diluting the purity of their disciplines. Therefore, faculty attitudes toward international learning affect their engagement in activities that further the implementation of their institutions' internationalization plans.

Personal knowledge and skills. Faculty who have lacked exposure to and involvement with different cultural perspectives may lack the knowledge and skills for how to engage in their institutions' internationalization plans. Specifically, faculty who have not (a) lived, worked, or traveled overseas or (b) had significant interactions with individuals from difference cultures in the US may lack an understanding necessary to integrate international and intercultural perspectives into their teaching and research (Bond, 2003; Green &

Olson, 2003). Faculty without significant international or intercultural experiences tend not to recognize the connections between the increasing importance of international knowledge and cross-cultural communication skills with their professional agendas. Therefore, by supporting faculty members' development of international knowledge and skills related to their disciplines, campus-wide committees can encourage faculty involvement in internationalization plans.

Cognitive competence. Even faculty who have had international experiences may lack the cognitive competence necessary not only to see the connections between these experiences and their teaching, research, and service, but to integrate this international knowledge into their work (Beltos, 1988; Ellingboe, 1998; Green & Olson, 2003; E. L. Miller, 1992). As Ellingboe (1998) observed, methods of infusing scholarship with international perspectives remain unknown even to some faculty with international experiences. Thus, specific intellectual, pedagogical, and assessment skills, other than those emphasized by faculty members' graduate training or disciplinary associations, may be necessary to enable faculty to infuse international content into their teaching and research. Therefore, it is important that internationalization leaders consider faculty members' awareness of the connections between their international experiences and their professional agendas in order to advance the implementation of their institution's internationalization plans.

In sum, despite the importance institutional leaders attribute to internationalization in their internationalization plans, significant institutional and individual barriers exist which hinder faculty involvement in internationalization initiatives. This study seeks to shed light on this problem through its investigation of the strategies used by campus-wide committees to overcome these barriers and effectively engage faculty in the operationalization of their institutions' internationalization plans.

Recommendations from Internationalization Leaders

Rewards and incentives are powerful tools for engaging faculty in international activities. As indicated in the NASULGC's Taskforce on International Education (2004) report, "Institutional recognition and support are a vital factor in increasing faculty international involvement" (p. 8). Thus, faculty are more likely to participate in internationalization plans if institutional policies facilitate their involvement through strategic incentives.

Internationalization experts concur on six overarching recommendations for institutions to encourage and reward faculty in internationalization. First, the inclusion of international scholarship and service in tenure and promotion policies provides critical incentives for faculty to integrate international per-spectives into their teaching, research, and service (Carter, 1992; Fischer, 2007; Gilliom, 1993; Green & Shoenberg, 2006; James & Nef, 2002; Knight, 2004; National Association of State Universities and Land Grant Colleges Task Force on International Education, 2004; Odgers & Giroux, 2006; Whal-ley, 1997). Backman (1981) advised that it is important to develop "a faculty reward system that does not penalize a faculty member for undertaking an overseas assignment" (p. 16). In order to implement this reward system, NASULGC (1993) suggested that institutions can "stop the tenure clock for junior faculty members on international assignments" (p. 8). As faculty tend to prioritize their professional agendas according to work that will advance their likelihood of obtaining tenure and promotions, if institutions seek to engage faculty in internationalization then it is important that their tenure and promotion policies reflect that institutional goal.

Second, the inclusion of international scholarship and service in faculty hiring guidelines is critical to developing a broad base of faculty champions and advocates for internationalization (Carter, 1992; Gray, 1977; Green & Shoenberg, 2006; National Association of State Universities and Land Grant Colleges, 1993). Thus, to encourage the internationalization of curricula, research, and service, it is advantageous for institutional leaders to take proactive measures to seek out faculty interested and experienced in those endeavors.

Third, a little funding goes a long way in encouraging faculty involve-ment in internationalization. As such, it is important to provide at least par-tial funding for faculty to conduct and present research overseas, as well as teach on international exchange programs (Backman, 1984; Bond, 2003; Carter, 1992; Chandler, 1999; Fischer, 2007; Fox, 1993; Gray, 1977). After evaluating institutional successes in comprehensive internationalization, Engberg and Green (2002) noted that faculty often return from overseas pro-fessional experiences with fresh enthusiasm and interest in international is-sues in their fields, which they communicate to colleagues. Therefore, even small amounts of financial resources can serve as springboards to promote greater faculty involvement in international activities.

A synthesis of promising internationalization practices noted in the na-tional studies conducted by ACE (Engberg & Green, 2002) and NAFSA (2003, 2004, 2005, 2006c, 2007) reveals that small amounts of institutional funding can be supplemented through strategic partnerships with higher edu-cation institutions in the US and overseas, private foundations, non-governmental organizations, and corporations to develop sufficient resources which faculty can engage in international activities. Through such strategic partnerships, institutions can support faculty in gaining experiences and networks to draw upon to internationalize their teaching, research, and service, and in so doing support the operationalization of their institutions' internationalization plans.

Fourth, it is helpful for institutions to provide curricular and pedagogical grants to support (a) the infusion of international content into existing courses and (b) the development of new courses with an international focus (Bond, 2003; Engberg & Green, 2002; Fischer, 2007; Harari, 1992; Johnston & Edelstein, 1993; National Association of State Universities and Land Grant Colleges Task Force on International Education, 2004). Even small amounts of funding, institutions can create incentives, such as through a curriculum development fund, for faculty to infuse international perspectives and content into their courses.

Fifth, in addition to providing curricular grants, faculty workshops on internationalizing curricula can provide opportunities for faculty to share their successful practices in redesigning curricula to integrate international and intercultural perspectives (Backman, 1984; Bond et al., 2003; Goodwin & Nacht, 1983; Green & Olson, 2003; E. L. Miller, 1992). These workshops serve as forums in which faculty can share examples of their international course units and syllabi.Yet, although these professional development programs may serve as useful mechanisms through which to empower faculty with the knowledge and skills necessary to internationalize their courses, research has indicated that faculty may resent the mere concept of "faculty development programs" and view any suggestion of the need for improvement as an insult to themselves and their mentors (Green & Olson, 2003; M. A. Miller, 2001). To address this challenge, Backman (1984) recommended

> internationalization leaders assure faculty that they, and they alone, are responsible for the content of their courses. They must decide how to best impart an international dimension to their courses. Suggestions can be made, of course, but attempting to dictate specifics may lead to further entrenchment and opposition. (p. 333)

Thus, campus-wide committees must be cognizant of both the utility and inherent challenges embedded in faculty development workshops to support widespread faculty participation in internationalization.

Sixth, it is critical that internationalization leaders on campus draw explicit connections between internationalization goals and processes with those of other campus-wide initiatives in which faculty are already engaged. For example, to promote faculty engagement in internationalization, it is constructive for institutional leaders to connect their internationalization plans with other institution-wide initiatives and forums, such as the faculty senate, curriculum committees, and disciplinary associations (Green & Olson, 2003; Green & Shoenberg, 2006; Olson et al., 2005, 2006). Through such a connective process, synergies between institutional priorities and organizational structures can be maximized, so that internationalization, a process that by definition strives to integrate an international or intercultural perspective into all institutional functions, can be advanced.

Despite all the aforementioned recommendations, how can a campus-wide committee know when widespread faculty engagement for internationalization has been developed? The presence of the following seven factors indicates the development of widespread faculty engagement in internationalization: (a) the development of a favorable attitude among at least 25% of the faculty toward integrating international perspectives into their teaching, research, and service; (b) the availability of international courses in disciplines throughout the campus, not just in one or two departments; (c) a high level of faculty involvement in international research and development activities; (d) the development of joint research projects between domestic and international colleagues that cross disciplinary and national borders; (e) a high percentage of faculty who travel abroad for scholarly purposes and return to their campuses to integrate their new international perspectives and knowledge into their curricula; (f) a high degree of faculty contact on campus with international students and visiting scholars; and (g) a high degree of faculty knowledge and utilization of the international research that exists on their campuses. In essence, the development of a critical mass of faculty supporters is key to integrating international perspectives into an institution's teaching, research, and service. Therefore, the presence of strategic institutional rewards and incentives advances the development of faculty engagement in internationalization and, in so doing, advances the implementation of an institution's internationalization plan.

Moreover, internationalization leaders indicate that the presence of strategic institutional rewards advances the development of faculty engagement in internationalization and, in so doing, advances the implementation of an institution's internationalization plan. This study builds on these expert practitioners' recommendations for faculty engagement in internationalization by examining how organizational practices—such as the offering of grants and workshops on internationalizing curricula, and the inclusion of international scholarship in tenure, promotion, and hiring guidelines—affected committees' development of widespread faculty involvement in operationalizing internationalization plans.

Chapter IV

Case Studies

Duke University and University of Richmond

This chapter presents individual case studies of two institutions that used concrete strategies to engage faculty in internationalization, as well as an analysis of findings across the two individual cases. Duke University and the University of Richmond were selected as exemplary cases to examine for multiple reasons: Both institutions are members of the Association of International Education Administrators (AIEA), which is an association of universities and colleges that are proactively seeking to internationalize (Association of International Education Administrators, 2009). Moreover, both institutions have written internationalization plans, developed internationalization committees, and highlighted faculty engagement as a key component of their internationalization. The data were obtained by methods including documentation, interviews, and focus groups. (See the Appendix for an explanation of the case study methodology.)

This chapter begins by presenting descriptive and demographic data about the two institutions investigated by this study—Duke University and the University of Richmond. Subsequently, individual case studies will be provided, followed by a presentation of cross-case findings and analysis. Finally, the cross-case analysis will synthesize the findings based upon the following topics: (a) context, (b) academic activities, (c) organizational practices, (d) organizational principles, and (e) types and alignment of internationalization plans that have affected faculty engagement in internationalization.

Descriptive and Demographic Information

Purposefully, study participants at Duke University and the University of Richmond included each university's AIEA representative, internationalization committee members, and two senior administrative leaders who were not members of this committee. In addition to conducting interviews and focus groups with the participants, data were collected through documentation. Table 1 displays the types and numbers of documents analyzed for this study.

Table 1. Types and Numbers of Documents Analyzed

Type of Documents	Number of Documents	
	Duke University	University of Richmond
Mission statement	1	1
Strategic plans that included internationalization[1]	13	3
Internationalization committee charge	1	1
Internationalization committee meeting minutes[2]	-	4
Internationalization committee annual reports	-	4
Faculty senate meeting minutes that addressed internationalization	9	-
Faculty program reports[3]	-	10
Institutional leader speeches, letters, presentations, and articles	5	4
Capital campaign case statements	1	1
Institution's web site documents[4]	46	55
External publications	8	7
Total documents analyzed	84	90

[1] At Duke University, strategic plans that included internationalization were the university strategic plans (2001, 2006), internationalization plans (1995, 2003), and all nine schools' 2006 strategic plans. At the University of Richmond, strategic plans that included internationalization included the university strategic plan (2000) and two internationalization plans (1986, 2006).

[2] The dash is used to indicate that relevant data were unavailable or did not exist.

[3] Faculty program reports refer to reports written by faculty members that detailed what they learned from the University of Richmond's faculty seminars abroad and, based on those experiences, their subsequent plans for internationalizing their curricula and research.

[4] Documents reviewed from the two institutions' Web sites include information on institutional history and demographics; international programs and centers; international research, teaching, and professional development funding opportunities; faculty tenure, promotion, and hiring policies; examples of internationalized syllabi; and campus newspaper and newsletter articles.

Case Study of Duke University

This section presents data collected on strategies used for engaging faculty in the operationalization of internationalization plans at Duke University. The main research question that framed the data collection and analysis was as follows: How has the development of faculty engagement affected the operationalization of internationalization plans? This main research question is operationalized through five subtopics, which examine the (a) context, (b) academic activities, (c) organizational practices, (d) organizational principles, and (e) types and alignment of internationalization plans that have affected faculty engagement in internationalization. This section is organized by these subtopics.

Context

This section on the context in which faculty engaged in the operationalization of internationalization plans at Duke University begins with background information, including the university's founding, school composition, and demographics. Next, the historical development of faculty engagement in internationalization plans at Duke will be explained briefly, followed by the supportive role the university's presidents have played in that development. Finally, the section will conclude with a summary of the contextual findings that affected faculty involvement in Duke University's internationalization plans.

Background

Located on 9,000 acres in Durham, North Carolina, "the City of Medicine,"[5] Duke University was founded in 1924 by James Buchanan Duke as a memorial to his father, Washington Duke (Duke University Office of News and Communications, 2007). The Duke family, which built a tobacco manufacturing empire and developed electricity production in the Carolinas, had been longtime supporters of Duke's antecedent school, Trinity College (Duke University Libraries, 2002). James Buchanan Duke's $40 million indenture transformed Trinity College, a regional liberal arts college into a national research university, which as of the end of the 2006 fiscal year possessed an endowment of $4.5 billion—the 16th largest higher education institutional endowment in the US (Duke University Office of News and Communications, 2007; National Association of College and University Business Officers, 2007).

---

[5] Durham, North Carolina was coined the "City of Medicine" in 1981 by the Chamber of Commerce to symbolize the city's transition from its focus on textiles and tobacco into an internationally renowned community of healthcare and medical science leaders (Duke University Medical Center Library and Archives, 2003).

A private research university, Duke University is comprised of nine schools, including the following, which are listed in order of establishment: Trinity College of Arts & Sciences (1859), School of Law (1904), Divinity School (1926), Graduate School (1926), School of Medicine (1930), School of Nursing (1931), Nicholas School of the Environment and Earth Sciences (1938), Pratt School of Engineering (1939), and Fuqua School of Business (1969) (Carnegie Foundation for the Advancement of Teaching, 2006a; Duke University Office of News and Communications, 2007). Descriptive and demographic information about Duke University is provided in Table 2.

Table 2. Descriptive and Demographic Information about Duke University

Institutional Characteristics of Duke University	
Year founded	1924
Location	Durham, NC
Geographic size	9,000 acres
Schools	Arts & Sciences Graduate School Business Law Engineering Medicine Environment Nursing Divinity
Institutional type	Private, research university
Endowment	$4.5 billion
National ranking of endowment	16th
Undergraduate students	6,197
Undergraduate students who are foreign nationals	6%
Graduate and professional students	6,627
Graduate students who are foreign nationals	22%
Students who study abroad	50%
Tenured or tenure-track faculty	1,667
Regular-rank faculty	997
Faculty who are foreign nationals	10%

Note. Data were derived from "Carnegie Classifications," by the Carnegie Foundation for the Advancement of Teaching; "Quick Facts about Duke University," by Duke University Office of News and Communication, 2007; "2006 NACUBO Endowment Study," by National Association of College and University Business Officers, 2007; and personal communications with Duke University administrators, August 17, 2007 and September 13, 2007.

Duke University has received national recognition for its internationalization practices. For example, Duke received the "Senator Paul Simon Award for Campus Internationalization" (NAFSA, 2004) and was a spotlighted school in NAFSA's (2003) "Internationalizing the Campus: Profiles of Success at Colleges and Universities" report. With national recognition for internationalization, a large endowment, a substantial percentage of students who study abroad or are foreign nationals, and three different types of internationalization plans, Duke University has been well poised to engage its faculty in internationalization.

Historical Context for Faculty Engagement in Duke's Internationalization Plans

In order to examine the strategies used to develop faculty engagement in Duke's internationalization plans, it is important to understand the historical context in which this engagement has taken place. In 1989, prompted by the fall of the Berlin Wall, a group of faculty approached the provost about the importance of internationalizing the curriculum (G. W. Merkx, personal communication, interview, May, 8, 2007). The provost responded by asking this multidisciplinary group to serve on the new "Provost's Executive Committee for International Affairs, [which he] charged with the mission of providing a plan of internationalization that could be integrated with Duke University's overall strategic plan" (Duke University Provost's Executive Committee for International Affairs, 1995, p. iii). After a year of work developing internationalization goals for the university, the faculty presented these goals to the provost, who responded by asking the faculty to develop a plan to implement those goals. As part of this internationalization plan development process, this committee canvassed faculty across the campus to learn about their international initiatives and interests. This faculty investigation led to the development of Duke's first internationalization plan, "Duke University in an Interdependent World," which the Provost's Executive Committee for International Affairs authored and the trustees adopted in 1994 (Duke University Provost's Executive Committee for International Affairs, 1995).[6]

Duke's first internationalization plan built upon the university's mission, which seeks "to advance the frontiers of knowledge and contribute boldly to the international community of scholarship [and] to promote a deep appreciation for the range of human difference and potential" (Duke University,

---

[6] This internationalization plan was originally published on February 17, 1994, revised on February 8, 1995, and updated on September 13, 1995. The internationalization plan referred to in this study is the September 13, 1995 updated version.

2001b, para. 1). Whereas Duke's mission laid out the institution's broad goals for internationalization, Duke's first internationalization plan created more specific goals and a road map for their operationalization.

In particular, Duke's 1995 internationalization outlined the following goals:

> to ensure that students, teachers, and the University community have the fullest opportunities to benefit in their teaching, training, performance, research, and personal growth from the broadest participation in the international system of culture and knowledge [and] be open to opportunities for pursuing and sharing international research, study, and experience, both on campus and abroad. (Duke University Provost's Executive Committee for International Affairs, 1995, p. iv)

In order to realize these goals, the plan articulated a series of steps, which were grouped into four categories: (a) undergraduate education, (b) graduate and professional education, (c) faculty development, and (d) university development. Because the plan advocated that "successful internationalization...will require both increasing the effective engagement of faculty with international interests and increasing the percentage of faculty who are internationally engaged" (p. vii), the following steps for faculty development were recommended:

1. Create a new initiatives pool to provide initial support for faculty ideas to internationalize their curricula, training, research, and outreach, including collaboration with other institutions in the US and abroad;

2. Increase funds for hiring new international faculty through additional support in the recruiting process to allow for interviewing foreign candidates and matching support to the schools for hiring new faculty in international studies;

3. Support opportunities for current faculty to enrich their international experiences and enhance the internationalization of their teaching and research;

4. Encourage and fund more foreign visiting scholars and practitioners, which will also improve collaboration with foreign institutions;

5. Advocate changes in rules and procedures regarding faculty hiring, tenure, and promotion that would underscore the importance the university accords to internationalization. (Duke University Provost's Executive Committee for International Affairs, 1995)

In addition to outlining the steps to develop faculty engagement in internationalization, the plan highlighted the benefits for such faculty involvement as follows:

1. Opportunities to undertake research and practice throughout the world, following the flow of intellectual development without undue practical obstacles;

2. Free and active participation in a fully international scholarly community;

3. Opportunities to bring international experiences and learning into the classroom, studio, and laboratory whenever and wherever appropriate. (Duke University Provost's Executive Committee for International Affairs, 1995, p. 3)

Significantly, Duke's first internationalization plan articulated the notion that "internationalization will succeed only if the faculty's interest in it is engaged and held, and solid benefits to research, performance, and teaching can be shown" (p. 11).

To operationalize this internationalization plan, Duke's president and provost committed significant resources and developed the Office of the Vice Provost for International Affairs, which brought internationalization into central academic planning (Duke University Provost's Executive Committee for International Affairs, 1995). These resources will be detailed in a subsequent section on Duke's substantial investments in internationalizationIn 2001, after an institution-wide strategic planning process, in which faculty and administrators throughout the university analyzed Duke's competitive advantages, constraints, opportunities, and resources, as they do every five years, the trustees approved a new university strategic plan, which established internationalization as one of Duke's nine major goals (Duke University, 2001a).[7] Internationalization had risen to the forefront of Duke's trustees and other senior institutional leaders' focus for the following reasons, as articulated in this 2001 university strategic plan, which was entitled "Building on Excellence":

> The end of the Cold War, the acceleration of globalization, and the pervasiveness of the internet have fundamentally altered the scope of universities' responsibilities, opportunities and challenges throughout the world. No longer can we prepare our students as if they are likely to pursue careers based in the United States, without much international contact or experience, and with little contact with colleagues from other nations and cultures. No longer can it be assumed that the best research

---

[7] In addition to advancing internationalization, Duke's "Building on Excellence" strategic plan (Duke University, 2001a) identified the following as institutional priorities: (a) build an excellent faculty in every school, (b) strengthen science and engineering, (c) integrate teaching, learning, and research, (d) promote interdisciplinary programs, (e) promote diversity, (f) intensify use of information technology, (g) promote students' civic engagement, and (h) build partnerships and collaborations in the local area, state, and beyond.

will be done in the United States and Europe and by scholars and researchers trained within our institutions. No longer is it the case that problems to which we apply our knowledge will be remote to our own concerns or that the solutions will be sought and sponsored primarily through government policies. These changes have profound implications for the international strategy of the University, with respect to its students, faculty and international reputation and presence. (pp. 64-65)

To address these challenges, Duke's 2001 strategic plan noted, "We acknowledge our responsibility to make internationalization an integrated part of undergraduate teaching, graduate and professional training, and faculty hiring" (p. 22). To accomplish this goal, the 2001 strategic plan outlined action steps related to faculty, international students, and study abroad. Given this study's focus on faculty, it is useful to examine the following steps related to faculty development:

- promote continuing internationalization of the faculty through the support of international research networks

- increase the annual allocation to library collections and place a higher priority on collection development for the international area

- expand the infrastructure support for information technology to ensure that the university's internationalization initiatives are technologically capable

- promote, as a university priority, a fundraising campaign goal of $20 million to replace and augment resources currently available for internationalization. (p. 91)

As such, the integration of internationalization into Duke's 2001 strategic plan reinforced the goals, resources, and support set forth in the 1995 internationalization plan for faculty to engage in international scholarship.

With the additional support provided by the establishment of internationalization as an official university priority in the 2001 strategic plan, Duke's vice provost for international affairs reported to the trustees in 2002 that the goals set forth in the first internationalization plan had been met. In response, the trustees charged the vice provost with developing an updated set of goals to advance the internationalization of the university (Duke University Provost's Executive Committee for International Affairs, 1995). This request from the trustees set in motion a year of collaborative meetings between the vice provost and the International Affairs Committee, which is a campus-wide group of faculty and administrators dedicated to the institution's internationalization, to develop Duke's second internationalization plan, "Raising the Bar: The Second Stage of Internationalization of Duke University" (Duke University Vice Provost for International Affairs and Development and International Affairs Committee, 2003). The International Affairs Committee had become the new incarnation of the Provost's Executive Committee on International Affairs, when the position of vice provost for international affairs was created in 1995. This committee was led by the vice provost for international affairs and included faculty and administrators with international focuses from each of Duke's schools, as well as administrators from Duke's central international offices, i.e. study abroad, visa, and area studies centers (Duke University Provost's Executive Committee for International Affairs, 1995). Together, the vice provost for international affairs and the International Affairs Committee authored Duke's 2003 internationalization plan.

The 2003 internationalization plan included updated goals and recommendations for faculty development. In particular, the 2003 plan identified that the four dimensions articulated in the 1995 plan, (a) undergraduate education, (b) graduate and professional education, (c) faculty development, and (d) university development, continued to represent the key internal categories through which Duke could deepen its international character. However, because these four dimensions were all internal in nature, the 2003 internationalization plan broadened its focus to address the external environment, as well. Accordingly, the 2003 internationalization plan added three new external dimensions of internationalization: "(e) national leadership and international recognition; (f) international partnerships with foreign institutions; and (g) cooperation for international development" (Duke University Vice Provost for International Affairs and Development and International Affairs Committee, 2003, p. 2).

Because the 2003 internationalization plan advocated that "the *sine qua non* of all Duke's international accomplishments is the faculty [and] without faculty, nothing is possible" (p. 15), the following faculty development goal was articulated: "develop and retain Duke's international faculty resources to sustain current achievements and undertake new selected initiatives" (p. 16). To operationalize this goal, the plan recommended that the university "continue to recognize achievement in international research and teaching as a dimension of excellence in tenure and promotion" and "provide the deans with an annual assessment of international faculty needs at the time that hiring plans are under development" (p. 16).

As part of the university's strategic plan renewal process every five years, Duke's commitment to internationalization was yet again advanced when the trustees adopted the next university strategic plan in 2006, "Making a Difference." Whereas Duke's 2001 strategic plan identified internationalization as one of nine institutional goals, Duke's 2006 strategic plan established internationalization as one of only six strategic priorities for the institution.[8] The rationale for Duke's trustees and other senior institutional leaders' focus on internationalization was explained as follows in the 2006 strategic plan:

> The events of September 11, 2001 and the subsequent invasion of Afghanistan and Iraq changed the world, dramatizing the religious, political, economic, cultural, military, and intellectual challenges that confront the rapidly globalizing, post-cold war world. These challenges have prompted nations, peoples, and institutions to consider more closely how they define themselves, and they have forced universities to frame new paradigms for research and education. Seeking to understand and thrive in this complicated new environment, Duke has increasingly focused on developing a sensitivity to, and awareness of, the fact that we operate in an interdependent world, where what were once hard and fast borders are now permeable, where individuals are part of an increasingly global community, and where problems transcend traditional boundaries. To be citizens of this world, we must be knowledgeable about issues that impact that world, such as global warming, poverty and pandemics, and conflicting cultures, and proactive in using that knowledge to make a difference. (p. 18)

To address these challenges, Duke's 2006 strategic plan set the following goals related to faculty engagement in internationalization: "target education and research resources to address significant and global issues; forge international partnerships to enhance education and research [and] focus resources on the recruitment, retention, and support of talented international faculty" (p. 18). Through the identification of internationalization as a renewed institutional priority in the university's 2006 strategic plan, Duke's institutional commitment to internationalization was reinforced.

What is more, in order to ensure implementation of the strategic plan's priorities, Duke's president and provost issued guidelines to the deans of Duke's nine schools to incorporate these priorities into their school strategic plans. This request prompted the schools' deans to commence discussions with their faculty to understand their international agendas and set internationalization goals related to their disciplines. As a result, all nine of Duke's schools incorporated internationalization into their 2006-2011 strategic plans (Duke Divinity School, 2006; Duke University Fuqua School of Business, 2006; Duke University Graduate School, 2006; Duke University Nicholas School of the Environment and Earth Sciences, 2006; Duke University Pratt School of Engineering, 2006; Duke University School of Law, 2006; Duke University School of Medicine, 2006; Duke University School of Nursing,

---

[8] In addition to internationalization, Duke's "Making a Difference" strategic plan (2006) included the following among its strategic priorities: (a) interdisciplinarity, (b) knowledge in the service of society, (c) centrality of the humanities and interpretive social sciences, (d) diversity, and (e) affordability and access.

2006; Duke University Trinity College of Arts & Sciences, 2006). The strategies for developing faculty engagement in internationalization, as advocated in each school's strategic plan, are addressed in a subsequent section on internationalization plans. These unit plans for internationalization will be discussed in greater depth in a subsequent section on the types and alignment of Duke's internationalization plans.

Duke has, therefore, infused internationalization into two university strategic plans (2001, 2006), developed two distinct internationalization plans (1995, 2003), and integrated internationalization into all nine schools' strategic plans (2006). In so doing, Duke has increased the visibility of internationalization as an institutional priority and allocated resources at various institutional levels to stimulate faculty involvement in international activities.

Supportive presidents. Duke's presidents have supported faculty involvement in the implementation of the institution's internationalization plans through both their rhetoric and commitment of resources. For example, Terry Sanford, former governor, senator, and Duke president from 1969 to 1985, encouraged faculty to set "outrageous ambitions" (Duke University Libraries, 2007, para. 11; Duke University Sanford Institute of Public Policy, 2007, para. 27; Sanford, 1984, para. 8), which set the stage for faculty to conceive internationalization as an "outrageous ambition" toward which to strive.

When Keith Brody assumed Duke's presidency in 1985, he created an important platform to support the operationalization of "outrageous ambitions" for Duke's internationalization: He expanded the perspectives represented on the board of trustees. According to Duke's Vice Provost for International Affairs Gilbert Merkx, "[President Brody] made the board [of trustees] more cosmopolitan and that really set the stage for...support for internationalization. He made it a truly national board " (personal communication, interview, August 17, 2007). Moreover, the fall of the Berlin Wall prompted President Brody to ask one of Duke's engineering professors from Eastern Europe to be Duke's unofficial ambassador in the former Soviet bloc countries. With a travel budget allocated by President Brody, this faculty ambassador "traveled extensively in Eastern Europe in the former Soviet bloc and set up a number of [institutional and faculty] connections" (G.W. Merkx, personal communication, interview, August 17, 2007). Thus, through President Brody's strategic expansion of the perspectives represented on Duke's board of trustees and specific charge to a faculty member to develop institutional and faculty connections in Eastern Europe, he created a foundation from which his successor could advance Duke's internationalization.

Subsequently, when Nannerl Keohane assumed the presidency in 1993, she expressed her focus on internationalization. In her inaugural address, she stated,

> We must cease to think of 'international' experiences as exotic, separate from our basic experience each day. We should make international links and contexts an integral part of the way we think and live at Duke; we should work past special enclaves and earmarked programs toward the day when everything we do will be informed by our global consciousness. (Keohane, 1993, p. 5)

President Keohane's emphasis on internationalization fueled the prevalent perception that "faculty either added to internationalization or were marginalized" (administrator, personal communication, focus group, May 3, 2007). According to Merkx, when President Keohane received Duke's first internationalization plan in 1995, she "decided to commit resources.... [So] the actual implementation of [Duke's internationalization plans] began under Nan Keohane's watch" (personal communication, interview, August 17, 2007). In particular, President Keohane and the provost each committed $300,000 a year to support faculty participation in international conferences and research, as well as to provide matching money for federal grants, which developed a foundation from which Duke's seven Title VI national resource center grants were awarded by the US Department of Education.[9]

President Keohane also oversaw a successful capital campaign from 1996 to 2003, which raised $2.36 billion, of which $9.9 million specifically earmarked for global initiatives (Duke University Office of News and Communications, 2007; Duke University Vice Provost for International Affairs and Development and International Affairs Committee, 2003). Accordingly, Duke's capital campaign case statement, which identified the campaign's funding priorities, included global initiatives (Duke University Office of Development, 1996). As such, President Keohane's leadership created an influx of resources with which faculty were encouraged to engage in international initiatives.

In 2004, a new leader, Richard Brodhead, assumed Duke's presidency. Participants expressed that President Brodhead has continued to support the internationalization programs and resources that were developed under President Keohane's leadership (G. Merkx, personal communication, inter-

---

[9]   Title VI national resource centers are competition and award based grants from the US Department of Education to higher education institutions to support "instruction in fields needed to provide full understanding of areas, regions or countries; research and training in international studies; work in the language aspects of professional and other fields of study; and instruction and research on issues in world affairs" (US Department of Education, 2007, para 1).

view, August 17, 2004; faculty member, personal communication, focus group, May 3, 2007). To illustrate this, a faculty member explained,

> I think that what Nan [Keohane] has started, Dick [Brodhead] has continued in having a very strong notion that Duke overseas needs to have a visible presence. [President Brodhead] was the first Duke president to come to the Arab world .... In several reports he gave to the board of trustees, he said, "One of my most interesting experiences was going to this desert kingdom called Qatar," and he described it. So, you can't pay for that. That just sort of does a ripple effect not only for the board of trustees but for the whole Duke community who reads the minutes of those meetings.... I think the current president, Dick Brodhead, very much continues and in some ways modifies what Nan [Keohane] did, but doesn't change the commitment to a broader international perspective. So, to have leadership with that attitude is extraordinary helpful, as a kind of psychological, not just programmatic, benefit. (personal communication, focus group, 2007)

Thus, President Brodhead's commitment to Duke's international academic activities through his travel and allocation of financial resources for such initiatives has led to psychological as well as programmatic support for faculty to engage in internationalization.

Overall, Duke's presidents have provided both symbolic and financial resources for faculty to engage in the implementation of the institution's internationalization plans. In particular, President Sanford's emphasis on outrageous ambitions, President Brody's broadening of the board of trustees and support for international exchanges, President Keohane's allocation of financial resources, and President Brodhead's continuing support have set the foundation from which the infrastructure to facilitate faculty engagement in Duke's internationalization has been created.

Unanticipated Factors

The important role that students have served in motivating Duke faculty to integrate international dimensions into their work was unanticipated, as it had not been revealed through an extensive literature review conducted for this study. Whereas administrators suggested in interviews that attendance at conferences overseas served as catalysts for faculty to add international dimensions to their work, which had been anticipated based on previous studies (e.g., Backman, 1984; Bond, 2003), numerous faculty highlighted in the focus group that their students' inquiries stimulated them to globalize their curricula, add international cases to their course discussions, explore international dimensions in their research, and advise students' international service projects through Duke's new civic learning initiative, which is known as "DukeEngage." For example, Vice Provost Merkx stated,

> I'm always amazed at how rewarding [professional experiences overseas are for] faculty members who are spending a long time in their lab or their home institution. Then you get them to go overseas and they go to a conference. They come back and they're just energized.... [about] that country and going abroad again. (personal communication, interview, May 8, 2007)

However, faculty emphasized the influence that students had upon internationalizing their teaching and research. For example, a faculty member pointed out that cross-cultural inquires from students have encouraged faculty to increase their knowledge of issues within their disciplines to include various countries and world regions' perspectives (personal communication, focus group, May 8, 2007). To exemplify what led faculty to internationalize their teaching, a faculty member explained, "One thing that happened was students would ask, 'How come we only use US cases?'" (personal communication, focus group, May 8, 2007).

This student influence also infiltrated Duke's first internationalization plan (1995) and the Fuqua School of Business strategic plan (2006). The first internationalization plan highlighted,

> Our students are also keenly aware of how important receiving an international education is for them. Many see their futures as creative participants in a globally bounded world. They are demanding new courses with traditional disciplines and stimulating faculty to look at topics from a more interdisciplinary perspective. (1995, p. 1)

The Fuqua School of Business 2006 strategic plan similarly articulated, "Many students...believe that we need to do much more to 'globalize' our curriculum" (p. 23). Hence, although administrators emphasized the importance of external factors, such as overseas conferences, in stimulating faculty to engage in international scholarship, faculty referred to an internal, institutional resource—their students—as a catalyst for their incorporation of international perspectives into their curricula and research.

Summary

In sum, this section detailed the context in which faculty engaged in internationalization at Duke University. The university's background was described, after which the historical development of Duke's two distinct internationalization plans (1995, 2003) internationalization plans and incorporation of internationalization into the university's two recent strategic plans (2000, 2006) were presented. The supportive role that Duke's presidents have served in developing faculty engagement in internationalization was also discussed. Finally, the unanticipated role that students have served in encouraging their faculty to integrate international perspectives into their classrooms and research was presented.

Academic Activities

In this section, academic activities that emerged from the data collection process as facilitators of faculty engagement in internationalization at Duke University will be presented. Academic activities encouraged faculty engagement in internationalization, by providing opportunities for faculty to add international perspectives to their teaching and research. Such academic activities included the development of faculty seminars, international degree programs, and an overseas medical school campus, which will be discussed in turn.

Faculty Seminars

Faculty seminars were identified as academic activities that provided useful forums for faculty to explore international dimensions in their teaching and research. These seminars and research clusters give faculty teaching release time to discuss a particular international theme with colleagues from numerous disciplines. A university administrator explained that such seminars "bring faculty together to [ask] 'What are our points of comparison?' And, there are resources to do that here [at Duke]". (personal communication, interview, May 8, 2007)

Another senior administrative leader added,

> Out of those seminars come curricular ideas, collaborative research grants and other things. At least what you get is an enhanced personal research agenda.... [The seminars] are places where faculty who might have only thought of themselves as tangentially interested can become much more deeply interested in these issues. (personal communication, interview, May 8, 2007)

Examples of these seminars that supported faculty to enhance their international scholarship include the Franklin Humanities Residential Seminar, Social Science Research Institute Faculty Fellows Seminar, South Asia Faculty Development Seminars, Symposium on Transcultural Humanities, and the Sawyer Seminar Program (Duke University Office of the Dean of Humanities, 2005; Duke University Trinity College of Arts & Sciences, 2006; NC Center for South Asia Studies, 2007). Some of the seminars specifically focus on helping faculty to draw on their international experiences in the classroom. A faculty member explained,

> We have what we call faculty development seminars that we offer through South Asia...We do this both internally and externally with neighboring universities. It

turns out that [North Carolina Central University has many faculty] who are described as international people, but don't use their international expertise in the classroom. So, we are actually having faculty development workshops, where we pay [faculty and] give them some time off to rethink how they can develop what they already have in their background to demonstrate pedagogically in the classroom. And, some of them find this pretty exciting. Some of them never thought that anyone really cared if they were from Turkey or Bangladesh. That is one of the ways to get people to self identify and project their own cultural resources, which they've taken for granted as something they can use curricularly. (personal communication, focus group, May 8, 2007)

Outcomes of these seminars frequently include newly developed international curricula and collaborative research grants (Senior administrative leader, May 8, 2007). For example, the Sawyer Seminar Program prompted faculty to develop international, interdisciplinary research projects, such as, "Human Being, Human Diversity and Human Welfare: A Cross-Disciplinary and Cross-Cultural Study in Culture, Science, and Medicine;" "Global Health and Social Justice;" "HIV-AIDS in Africa, Haiti, and North Carolina; Portents and Dilemmas: Public Health and the Environment in China and India" (Davidson, 2006). Hence, such seminars provided infrastructural support through which faculty could explore international dimensions of their research and teaching.

International Degree Programs

Likewise, international degree programs were highlighted as academic activities that stimulated faculty to engage in international teaching at Duke University. International degree programs are undergraduate, graduate, and professional degrees offered by the institution that have a transnational or comparative focus. Through participation in international degree programs, faculty were prompted to develop and teach international curricula, as well as engage in classroom discussions with internationally focused students. Such degree programs include the Duke University/Frankfurt University Executive MBA, Duke Global Executive MBA, and JD/LLM in Comparative and International Law (Duke University Fuqua School of Business, 2007a, 2007b, 2007c; Duke University School of Law, 2006, 2007b, 2007d; Sheppard & Wahrenburg, 2007).

To elucidate how these international degree programs have developed faculty engagement in international scholarship, a faculty member explained,

In 1995 we announced the Global Executive MBA Program. Students come from all over the world and...meet their faculty first at Duke, and then in Europe, and then China, and then Latin America. And, it was really as a result of the pressure from the students that the faculty teaching in Latin America, China, and Europe began to [commit themselves to developing] knowledge about different areas. As a result, the courses began to change because they were more relevant to the region of teaching. As we rotated faculty through that program, we began to develop an internal group faculty that developed an international appreciation. They are not formally trained, but we began to develop international interests. (personal communication, focus group, May 3, 2007)

As this example highlights, international degree programs have provided avenues through which Duke faculty not only have developed and taught international curricula, but have engaged in ongoing discussions about international issues within their disciplines with students.

Development of an Overseas Campus

The development of a medical campus overseas, the Duke University-National University of Singapore Graduate Medical School, has provided opportunities for faculty to participate in international teaching, research, and curriculum development. This collaboration between Duke University and the National University of Singapore began in 2003 when "the Singaporean Ministry of Education approached Duke about [partnering to create Singapore's first graduate medical school] because of [the Duke] Medical Center's renowned reputation and [the Duke] School of Medicine's distinctive educational program, its research activity and faculty resources" (Duke University Medical Center, 2003, para. 6). Since the establishment of this joint initiative in 2005, Duke medical and science faculty have been presented with opportunities and funding to engage in collaborative research projects with the National University of Singapore (NUS) faculty (Bliwise, 2005). In a letter to the Duke University School of Medicine community, the school's dean, R. Sanders Williams, described,

> This affiliation [provides] opportunities for collaborative research, particularly patient-oriented research, that otherwise would not be open to our faculty…. In the longer term, collaborations between Singaporean and Duke faculty should generate new funding for notable science. (2007, para. 6)

As such, this overseas campus collaboration has also enabled faculty to experiment with fresh approaches to enhance their research and curricula.

In illustration of the significant support that this overseas campus has provided for faculty to engage in international research, Dean Williams explained in an article in Duke University Medical Center & Health System employee newsletter,

> The government of Singapore is investing over 300 million dollars in this project. Much of that will support research which will be done by Duke faculty affiliated

with the GMS in Singapore. Other research will involve collaborations between the
GMS and Duke. (M. Green, 2005)

Furthermore, in this newsletter, Victor Dzau, Duke University's chancellor
for health affairs added,

Singapore has made a vast commitment to becoming a leader in biomedical
research. The opportunity to form collaborations in this environment will help us
accelerate our efforts in the area of transnational research, which is a strategic
priority for Duke Medicine. (M. Green, 2005)

Thus, the development of this medical campus overseas has provided a
foundation for Duke faculty to engage in research and teaching on prominent
healthcare issues in Singapore and in Asia, as well as pursue transnational,
biomedical research, thereby promoting their involvement with international
scholarship, and as a result, the advancement of their university's
internationalization plans.

Summary

In sum, three overarching types of academic activities—faculty seminars,
international degree programs, and the development of an overseas medical
school campus—were used at Duke University to develop faculty
engagement in internationalization. Table 3 details these academic activities
and includes examples.

Table 3. Duke's Academic Activities Used to Develop Faculty Engagement
in Internationalization

Strategy	Examples
Faculty seminars	Franklin Humanities Residential Seminar Social Science Research Institute Faculty Fellows Seminar South Asia Faculty Development Seminars Symposium on Transcultural Humanities Sawyer Seminar Program
International degree programs	Duke University/Frankfurt University MBA Duke Global Executive MBA JD/LLM in Comparative and International Law
Overseas medical school campus	Duke University/National University of Singapore Graduate Medical School

Organizational Practices

In this section, organizational practices that emerged from the data collection process, which affected faculty engagement in internationalization at Duke University, will be presented. Organizational practices refer to the policies, structures, and actions usually initiated by senior administrative leaders that affect faculty work. Organizational practices encouraged faculty engagement in internationalization, by providing critical infrastructure, incentives, and communication mechanisms to support faculty in developing international dimensions in their teaching and research. Organizational practices included Duke's substantial investments in internationalization, strategic use of electronic resources, development of international centers, and reaccreditation self-study. However, the lack of inclusion of internationalization in Duke's tenure and promotion policies emerged as an obstacle that limited the engagement of some faculty in international scholarship. These organizational practices will be discussed in turn.

Substantial Investments in Internationalization

Duke has made substantial financial investments to support faculty engagement in international initiatives. These financial commitments include (a) differential investment, (b) multiple distinguished international scholar endowments, (c) curriculum internationalization grants, and (d) the Office of the Vice Provost for International Affairs (OVPIA) international research and travel funds.

Differential investment. "Differential investment" is a term used at Duke to refer to the process of allocating special funds for initiatives that promote strategic plan priorities (Senior administrative leaders, personal communications, interviews, May 8, 2007; electronic mail, August 27, 2007). Duke's Trinity College of Arts and Sciences 2006 strategic plan explained, "We will make differential investment in a limited number of thematic areas...rather than department by department" (p. 15).

To clarify the rationale for differential investment, Duke's 2006 strategic plan articulated,

> Our planning has highlighted a number of ongoing priorities and critical new investments in programs and facilities that we must support financially if the plan is to succeed.... While our schools have considerable latitude in prioritizing expenditures and strong incentives to generate funds and allocate them wisely, we have also developed strong central funding mechanisms to supplement school resources to achieve critical priorities. (p. 67)

Differential investment in Duke's strategic plan priorities is supported by the parallel "strategic investment plan," which

> [underwrites] the implementation of the university strategic plan, providing a clear guide to priorities, and a resource allocation blueprint for program support and capital projects.... Our general expectation is that programmatic support from central funds will not continue beyond five years; funding will shift either to external grants and contracts, new endowment income, or the budgets of the schools. Programmatic support is thus a form of bridge funding. (Duke University, 2006, p. 69)

As Duke's 2006 strategic plan identified internationalization as one of its six institutional priorities, substantial resources have been allocated throughout the institution for faculty to engage in internationalization.

To operationalize Duke's internationalization plans, faculty have been given incentives by schools and institutional centers to pursue research and teaching initiatives that promote internationalization themes. A senior administrative leader shed light onto how differential investment affected faculty involvement in the internationalization of Duke's Trinity College of Arts & Sciences:

> As we were thinking about major [internationalization] themes that we wanted to invest in differentially, [two themes] emerged...Global health is one. Given our medical center, given our social sciences, the combination does make great sense that we would make a major investment in global health...The second is something that affects humanities and the social sciences and that is "transcultural perspectives" ...How [is] it that cultures connect and how [is] it they evolve? So, we can have a number of disciplines with faculty looking at that question from different perspectives. (personal communication, interview, May 8, 2007)

For example, to encourage faculty involvement in Duke's internationalization themes, faculty are eligible for $5,000 travel awards from Duke's Center for International Studies and Global Health Institute to conduct research that addresses global health through the lens of any disciplinary framework (Duke University Center for International Studies, 2007). For example, in 2007, faculty from a variety of disciplines, including public policy, nursing, and environmental sciences, received these awards to conduct research respectively on orphanhood in India, cardiovascular disease management in the Caribbean, and social factors in malaria control in Tanzania (administrator, personal communication, electronic mail, November 1, 2007). Thus, through differential investment, Duke has allocated special funding through individual schools and centers to support faculty engagement in internationalization initiatives.

Multiple distinguished international scholar endowments. Furthermore, through the multiple university endowments to bring distinguished international scholars to Duke, faculty have developed communications with leading scholars from other countries. Such endowments have enabled faculty to gain insights into their disciplines from a variety of national and regional perspectives. These endowments include the Karl von der Heyden International Fellows Program Endowment, Semans Professorship for Distinguished International Visiting Scholars Endowment, and the Bernstein Memorial International and Comparative Law Endowment (Duke University Office of the Vice Provost for International Affairs & Development, 2005f; Duke University School of Law, 2002).

Curriculum internationalization grants. Curriculum development awards offered by Duke's Title VI centers have served two important functions in developing faculty engagement in international scholarship. First, they have provided support for faculty who are already internationalizing their courses. Second, they have provided faculty who have not integrated international components into their curricula with an incentive to do so (Asian/Pacific Studies Institute at Duke University, 2007a; Duke Center for Latin American and Caribbean Studies, 2007b). For example, Duke's Asian/Pacific Studies Institute has provided $3,000 grants for faculty to develop courses that have at least 35% East Asian (i.e., Chinese, Japanese, Korean, and Taiwanese) content and will be taught at least twice in the next five years (Asian/Pacific Studies Institute at Duke University, 2007a). In addition, the Office of Study Abroad's "Curriculum Integration Initiative" has provided incentives for faculty to integrate study abroad into their courses, including financial awards to departments for course developments and to individual faculty members for their site visits to overseas partner institutions and conference attendance (administrator, personal communication, electronic mail, July 27, 2007).

OVPIA international research and travel funds. The OVPIA has functioned like an "internal foundation," which supports faculty involvement in international activities (G. W. Merkx, personal communication, interview, May 8, 2007). Through the vice provost's office, faculty have received matching grants for international research proposals. Moreover, the international travel grants provided by this office have afforded faculty opportunities to attend conferences, conduct research, and pursue service projects overseas (G. W. Merkx, personal communication, interview, May 8, 2007).

Summary. As indicated, Duke's substantial investments in internationalization have supported faculty involvement in international activities. First, the practice of differential investment has provided resources for faculty to engage in the internationalization initiatives indicated in Duke's strategic plans. Second, multiple distinguished international scholar endowments have provided avenues through which Duke faculty have gained insights into various national and regional perspectives on their disciplines. Third, curriculum internationalization grants have provided financial incentives for faculty to internationalize their courses. Finally, the OVPIA has provided resources for faculty to conduct research overseas.

Strategic Use of Electronic Resources

Strategic use of electronic resources by the Office of the Vice Provost for International Affairs (OVPIA) has supported faculty awareness of opportunities to engage in the implementation of Duke's internationalization plans. In particular, through the OVPIA's purposeful use of the university's Web site, including the international faculty database and international blogs, centralized access points have been created through which faculty have gained information on opportunities to engage in international teaching, research, and service.

The international portal of Duke's Web site, known as the "Global Gateway," has served as a centralized mechanism to inform faculty of international opportunities (Duke University Office of the Vice Provost for International Affairs & Development, 2005g). This Global Gateway also houses Duke's international faculty database and international blogs, which support faculty involvement in international initiatives. Through this database, faculty search for colleagues engaged in research on specific topics, countries, or regions (Duke University Office of the Vice Provost for International Affairs & Development, 2005a). As an important component of international scholarship is collaboration across nations and disciplines, this database enables faculty to identify and promptly contact knowledgeable colleagues about international matters of specific interest.

Further, opportunities to develop international blogs posted on the Global Gateway and provide faculty with venues to share their international teaching, research, and service opportunities with each other, thus promoting support and awareness of the international engagements of Duke faculty (Duke University Office of the Vice Provost for International Affairs & Development, 2005b). Specifically, Duke's Global Health Institute Web page has provided a blog forum for Duke medical faculty to share their engagement in global health service projects, such as their training of Ugandan surgeons on new equipment used for brain and spinal procedures (Duke University School of Medicine, 2007). Hence, the OVPIA's strategic use of electronic resources, including the international faculty blogs and database on its Web page, has provided a centralized portal through which faculty have shared and gained access to international resources to advance their scholarly agendas and, in so doing, advance Duke's internationalization plans.

Development of International Centers

Duke's seven Title VI national resource centers[10] awarded by the US Department of Education and over a dozen additional international and area studies centers have served as focal points for faculty to engage in intellectually stimulating research and teaching initiatives across disciplinary boundaries and world regions (Duke University Office of the Vice Provost for International Affairs & Development, 2005d, 2005e). As aforementioned, Title VI national resource centers were established at Duke through grants from the US Department of Education to support teaching and research in particular world regions (US Department of Education, 2007). Duke's Title VI and other international and area studies centers have provided faculty support in the form of research grants, curriculum development awards, working groups, research clusters, exchange programs, and conferences at Duke through which faculty can expand their international foci or connections (Duke University Office of the Vice Provost for International Affairs & Development, 2005e).

These centers have provided resources for faculty to incorporate international content into their courses and research agenda. For example, the Asian/Pacific Studies Institute has sponsored faculty workshops and research on environmentalism, gender and rural development in transitional economics in the Asian/Pacific region (Asian/Pacific Studies Institute at Duke University, 2007b). In addition, the John Hope Franklin Center for Interdisciplinary and International Studies has provided videoconferencing technology for faculty to incorporate into their curricula real-time discussions with scholars overseas (John Hope Franklin Center for Interdisciplinary and International Studies at Duke University, 2007b). Above all, the centers have supported faculty engagement in international initiatives by incubating interdisciplinary collaborations in various world regions (e.g., Asian/Pacific Studies Institute at Duke University, 2007b; Duke Center for Latin American and Caribbean Studies, 2007a).

---

[10] Duke's Title VI national resource centers include the (a) Asian/Pacific Studies Institute, (b) Center for European Studies, (c) Center for International Business Education & Research, (d) Center for International Studies, (e) Center for Latin American & Caribbean Studies, (f) Center for Slavic, Eurasian & East European Studies, and (f) North Carolina Center for South Asia Studies (Duke University Office of the Vice Provost for International Affairs & Development, 2005d, 2005e).

Reaccreditation Self-Study

In 1998, preparation for Duke's reaccreditation through the Southern Association of Colleges and Schools prompted faculty to examine their core undergraduate curriculum and recognize that the core curriculum was not preparing students to navigate and participate in different regional and national cultures. To illustrate this point, a senior administrative leader reflected,

> Our last reaccreditation through the Southern Association of Colleges and Schools led to recognition that...there was no formal language requirement. Is that good preparation for functioning in a complex world? The answer was pretty obviously, no.... So, here you have one of those unique situations where all the faculty could step back and say "Yes, it's broken. This is not good." That was an amazing outcome of the self-study. It was [a] general recognition that we could and should do better than we were doing to prepare our students.... [Faculty] understood, whether you're talking regionally or nationally or internationally that relations among cultures and being able to navigate, negotiate, and participate [in different cultures] was fundamental. So, [developing the cross-cultural inquiry curriculum requirement] wasn't a hard sell. You had some arguing about the specifics, but not about the idea. (personal communication, interview, May 8, 2007)

After the yearlong series of discussions, Duke's Trinity College of Arts & Sciences faculty decided to organize the core curriculum for undergraduate students according to seven critical modes of inquiry,[11] two of which were "cross-cultural inquiry" and "foreign languages" (Duke Trinity College of Arts and Sciences, 2007). As a result of the self-study, this senior administrative leader explained,

> We changed the curriculum to require two courses that we call "Cross-Cultural Inquiry" [and] we inserted a language requirement.... Those are substantial steps to change the infrastructure and to prepare students for the roles we envisioned for them.... If you're talking about crossing cultures, you have to have the tools in your toolbox. Language is one tool, but learning how to understand and appreciate cultures was part of the other aspects, so that's why [we developed] the cross-cultural inquiry [and foreign language requirements]. (personal communication, interview, May 8, 2007)

In addition to restructuring the core curriculum to emphasize cross-cultural inquiry and foreign languages, Duke faculty established learning outcomes and assessment mechanisms to evaluate the new curriculum on descriptive, analytical, and experimental levels (Thompson & Williard, 2003). In particu-

---

[11] In addition to cross-cultural inquiry and foreign languages, the revised core curriculum that emerged from the 1998 reaccreditation self-study required students to complete courses emphasizing five other modes of inquiry: (a) ethical inquiry, (b) science, technology, and society, (c) research, (d) writing, and (e) quantitative, inductive, and deductive reasoning

lar, faculty defined specific core learning outcomes in terms of (a) intellectual skills (e.g., critical thinking and reasoning) and (b) broad dispositions and understandings (e.g., cross cultural fluency). Faculty enabled themselves to evaluate these learning outcomes through tracking students' curricular choices and relating learning outcomes to student variables, experience patterns, and course and faculty characteristics (Thompson & Williard, 2003). As such, the reaccreditation self-study served as a catalyst for faculty to integrate cross-cultural education into the core curriculum, by providing an opportunity for faculty to analyze how the curriculum was and is continuing to prepare students to function in a complex world with increasing cross-cultural interactions.

Lack of Inclusion of Internationalization in Tenure and Promotion Policies

The lack of an explicit inclusion of international scholarship into Duke's tenure and promotion policies emerged as an organizational practice that hindered the involvement of faculty, particularly junior faculty, in international initiatives. Duke's first internationalization plan noted,

> Discussions with faculty from several schools and departments revealed that junior faculty in some fields are convinced that international research, teaching, and engagement do not receive the same recognition from the departmental level upwards in promotion and tenure decisions as accomplishments in domestic and/or theoretical subject areas." (1995, p. 13)

In further illustration of this point, a faculty member indicated,

> I've gone through [the tenure process with] four or five individuals in the last seven years where the international component has been there, but doesn't count as much as a published monograph or a series of refereed articles. But, if it can be shown that it is additive and in some way contributes to not only the recognition, but the academic excellence of the individual concerned, then one can make that case. But, it's always going to be second, until [the tenure policy explicitly incorporates and rewards international scholarship]. (personal communication, focus group, May 8, 2007)

A university administrator added, "We need...ways of getting our younger faculty engaged [in international initiatives] early enough that they don't feel as if their tenure is threatened" (personal communication, focus group, May 8, 2007).

Duke's second internationalization plan, however, maintained the adequacy for excellence in scholarship to remain the sole criterion for tenure and promotion decisions due to the value of internationalization embedded into Duke's organizational culture:

Duke's promotion and tenure policies make no mention of international teaching, research, or service, reflecting Duke's emphasis on maintaining excellence as the only criterion on which tenure decisions are to be judged. Fortunately, recognition of international achievement in Duke's promotion and tenure review processes does not require changing the criterion of excellence or revising promotion and tenure policy. To the extent that international teaching and scholarship are valued as part of the Duke mission, they will be given weight at each level of the promotion and tenure processes. The changes in institutional culture that have taken place over the last decade have gone far to address the junior faculty concerns mentioned in the [1995 internationalization plan. (Duke University Vice Provost for International Affairs and Development and International Affairs Committee, 2003, p. 16)

Yet, despite the organizational shift noted in Duke's second internationalization plan, the focus group and interviews conducted for this study revealed that the lack of integration of international scholarship into Duke's tenure and promotion policies remains an obstacle that inhibits some faculty from engaging in international initiatives.

Table 4. Duke's Organizational Practices Used to Develop Faculty Engagement in Internationalization

Strategy	Examples
Substantial investments in internationalization	Differential investment
	Multiple distinguished international scholar endowments
	Curriculum internationalization grants
	OVPIA international research and travel grants
Strategic use of electronic resources	International portal on university Web site
	International faculty database
	International blogs
Development of international centers	Asian/Pacific Studies Institute
	John Hope Franklin Center for Interdisciplinary and International Studies
	Duke Center for Latin American and Caribbean Studies
Reaccreditation self-study	1989 Southern Association of Colleges and Schools self-study

Summary

In sum, the organizational practices used at Duke University to develop faculty engagement in internationalization include substantial investments in internationalization, strategic use of electronic resources, development of international centers, and reaccreditation self-study (see Table 4). However, one organizational practice emerged that hindered the involvement of junior faculty in internationalization: the lack of inclusion of international scholarship in Duke's tenure and promotion policies.

Organizational Principles

In this section, the organizational principles that emerged organically at each institution as facilitators of faculty engagement in internationalization will be presented. Organizational principles refer to accepted codes of conduct that guide faculty teaching, research, and service. The principles of collaboration, interdisciplinarity, customization, coordination, and entrepreneurship encouraged faculty to participate in international initiatives at Duke University, and will be discussed in turn.

Collaboration

The principle of collaboration highlights the necessity of working jointly with colleagues for mutual benefit. Through a "history and ethos of collaboration" in Duke's institutional culture, faculty have been encouraged and supported to develop joint projects on international topics with overseas and US institutions (Senior administrative leader, personal communication, interview, May 8, 2007). This senior administrative leader continued, "By creating more collaboration, [joint] initiatives grow, [so that faculty] bring together all the little grassroots bits and pieces that have been out there and figure out how they can best work together" (personal communication, interview, May 8, 2007).

According to Duke's current president, Richard Brodhead, this emphasis on collaboration is not only a component of Duke's past and present, but future, as well. On Duke's strategic plan Web site, President Brodhead emphasized, "While Duke will continue to embrace the essential aspects of specialized research, teaching and learning, the university will build on its special strengths in collaboration and connection of knowledge to real-world problems" (2006, para. 4). As collaboration emerged as a bedrock of the 2006 university strategic plan, which identified internationalization as one its priorities, internationalization as an institutional priority and collaboration as a guiding principle were intertwined in Duke's internationalization plans and their implementation.

This institutional focus on collaboration was advocated by another senior administrative leader who described,

> The collaborations that go on, the interactions that go on, are not confined to your hallway anymore. We really have a much different scope. I think that it's really advantageous here.... We will intentionally seek to develop collaborative relationships with institutions. I think that makes a big difference.... Our faculty have multiple connections with foreign or international institutions and colleagues. It is in every discipline and I think it is the nature of disciplines, some more than others, but none are excluded from this process of being worldwide engagements. So certainly, faculty with the stature that we have at Duke participate in those disciplinary international conversations [and] collaborative relationships. People tend to think of it in the sciences, but it extends past the sciences into each of the other the divisions, [including] social sciences and humanities. (personal communication, interview, May 8, 2007).

As indicated by this senior administrative leader and President Brodhead, collaboration has been an important component of Duke's institutional ethos. Consequently, as Duke has developed its internationalization plans, the organizational principle of collaboration has extended to international collaborations.

Duke's emphasis on collaboration was grounded in the university's first internationalization plan (1995), which recommended "increasing the percentage of faculty who are internationally engaged [by].... creating a New Initiatives Pool to provide initial support for faculty ideas in curriculum, training, research, performance, and outreach including collaborations with other institutions in the United States and abroad" (p. vii). This plan continued,

> We recommend that funds to support this effort (about $30,000 annually) be drawn from the New Initiatives Pool, particularly to encourage faculty to undertake new projects or exchanges with target institutions. One major objective here is to form durable relationships on which future collaborative projects, from different areas of the University, can be built. (1995, p. 13)

Thus, financial resources for faculty to engage in international collaborations were allocated through Duke's 1995 internationalization plan. In particular, the 1995 internationalization plan's collaborative recommendations have been operationalized through the development of numerous international centers, faculty seminars, and Duke's medical campus in Singapore, which have provided financial and infrastructural support for faculty to engage in international collaborations.

Interdisciplinarity

Interdisciplinarity was an organizational principle that opened the doors to international engagement for many faculty at Duke. According to Cathy Davidson (2006), Duke's former vice provost for interdisciplinary affairs, interdisciplinarity is any productive research or teaching that occurs across, between, or among two or more areas of knowledge that typically have different histories, methodologies, or objects of study. Interdisciplinarity can occur across schools or it can happen within a single department; it can involve collaborations of many researchers or it can be embodied in the work of a single researcher (pp. 1-2).

Interdisciplinarity has long been a prominent principle within Duke's institutional culture, as emphasized by Duke's recent presidents, 1987 accreditation review, 1995 internationalization plan, 2006 university strategic plan, 2006 Trinity College of Arts and Sciences strategic plan, and 2006 School of Law strategic plan. Davidson (2006) explained,

> Interdisciplinarity has been a hallmark at Duke at least since 1970 when Duke created the Department of Biomedical Engineering.... Many educational commentators, watching Duke's almost unprecedented rise from a regional university to one of the great universities in the country, point to *the extent, depth, and history of our interdisciplinarity as a significant factor in the rapid growth in our reputation, respect, and influence.* As part of the strategic planning process, we have embraced the uniquely widespread interdisciplinarity of our campus and consciously worked on creating structures and infrastructures that support the flow of ideas from one end of campus to another.... We believe that we help facilitate excellent research and teaching by making institutional structures flexible and amenable to work that occurs outside the traditional definitions of departments, schools, and disciplines.... We believe that the most successful interdisciplinarity is a process of new questions, methods, and insights coming out of and flowing back into disciplines. (pp. 1-2)

A senior administrative leader concurred,

> One of the things that has been part of Duke's identity is interdisciplinarity. Duke was interdisciplinary way before that became a common coin. It was interdisciplinary not just within schools, but across schools. Part of that had to do with the proximity. So we are fortunate that on one campus we have all of our schools. It's not like our medical school is fifty miles away.... We have the same school and department structure that everyone else has, but we've developed this structure to facilitate interdisciplinary team approaches around particular problems. So, we have many interdisciplinary centers and these do cut across schools as well as within schools.... These have been really fundamental in promoting the type of collaborations that [encourage faculty to bring] multiple disciplines and perspective to bear. With our faculty involved internationally, then it just by definition beings those other perspectives to bear. (personal communication, interview, May 8, 2007)

Emphasis on interdisciplinarity in Duke's strategic and internationalization plans. Commitment to interdisciplinarity is grounded in the university's strategic and internationalization plans. Duke's first internationalization plan (1995) identified, "The University can profit both by assisting development of new courses with international focus or content, and by encouraging new orientations for existing courses. In either case comparative and interdisciplinary studies and methods should be encouraged" (p. 12). To do so, the plan advocated "furnishing multidisciplinary opportunities that are complementary to the University's own strengths and resources" (1995, p. 16). Such multidisciplinary opportunities for faculty were created through Duke's international and interdisciplinary centers, e.g., the John Hope Franklin Center for Interdisciplinary and International Studies, Global Health Institute, and Center for South Asian Studies, as well as the faculty seminars sponsored by these centers.

Duke's current university strategic plan (2006) reinforced this goal:

> Many of the most interesting and pressing problems of today, such as environmental pollution or economic competitiveness, human health or cultural understanding, are deeply interdisciplinary at their core.... Faculty... who are equipped to address these issues most constructively will be those who have learned to work in more than one dimension, using the tools of their own as well as other disciplines, who have been trained to grasp the interaction of many parts of the question and bring to bear multiple sets of analytic skills, and who can collaborate as well as work alone. Duke has long recognized this fact, and perhaps our best known institutional strength is our self-definition as a scholarly community that values, and has a proven track-record of success with, interdisciplinarity. Interdisciplinarity thrives at Duke because faculty tend to be less oriented to a map of the disciplines than to intellectual questions and living human issues, which their knowledge might help to understand. When we are oriented toward challenges of this order, the disciplines are naturally synergistic, since no discipline holds all the pieces of the puzzle to be solved. As a young university, we have been forced to leverage resources and collaborate across departmental and school boundaries, a feat facilitated by our compact campus that joins in close proximity—unlike many other major research universities—our undergraduate, graduate, and professional schools. (p. 15)

Duke's Trinity College of Arts and Sciences' strategic plan (2006) similarly advocated for faculty's emphasis on interdisciplinarity and internationalization by seeking to

> insure that members of the arts faculty are engaged in planning for the Global Health Initiative....[by] amplifying the cross-disciplinary, cross-divisional, and cross-professional conversations that have already begun to make Duke a leader in new models of scholarship designed to study and improve the human condition. (p. 44)

Likewise, the School of Law's strategic plan (2006) emphasized the importance of faculty involvement in scholarship that is both interdisciplinary and international:

> The international and comparative law faculty routinely engage in scholarly collaboration, faculty workshops, and conferences across schools and departments across campus. Among the most active ongoing collaborations are those with the Political Science Department, the Sanford Institute of Public Policy, the Fuqua School of Business, and various area studies programs. Much of Duke's distinction in [international and comparative law] can be credited to the interdisciplinary character of the University overall. (p. 14)

Duke faculty members' value of interdisciplinarity created an important foundation from which to initiate their involvement in international teaching and research. As interdisciplinarity emphasizes comparative approaches, this organizational principle has served as a launching pad for faculty to advance their interdisciplinary scholarship through the integration of international and cross-cultural perspectives.

Support for faculty to build international components into their interdisciplinary teaching and research agendas has been provided by centers, such as the John Hope Franklin Center for Interdisciplinary and International Studies, and the Global Capital Markets Center, which is a collaborative undertaking of Duke's Law School and Fuqua School of Business that promotes interdisciplinary teaching and research on world capital markets (Duke University School of Law, 2006; John Hope Franklin Center for Interdisciplinary and International Studies at Duke University, 2007a, 2007b). As such, interdisciplinarity is a seminal organizational principle that has buttressed faculty engagement in scholarship at the boundaries of various disciplines and cultures.

Customization

The principle of customization emphasizes the value of adapting institution's internationalization goals to departments' disciplinary priorities and individual faculty members' scholarly interests. The principle of customization fueled the development of an internationalization section in each school's strategic plan, which in turn, related internationalization goals and opportunities to faculty members' disciplines (G. W. Merkx, personal communications, interviews, May 8, 2007; August 17, 2007). By customizing the internationalization plans to each discipline, the connections between disciplinary priorities and internationalization were made explicit. Customization of internationalization plans is particularly important, as Duke's internationalization plan (2003) indicates: *"Faculty participation in [internationalization] only takes place when faculty themselves find it useful. It cannot be coerced"* (p. 25).

Merkx advanced the importance of customization as he explained,

> In the previous [university] strategic plan...internationalization was one of eight priorities for the university as a whole, but it wasn't integrated. It did not appear in all of the plans in all of the schools. This time [the president and provost said every school must] have a section on internationalization.... because it's one of the [university's strategic plan] themes....So, all the schools did that. It had several effects. One is it made [all the schools] think about [internationalization]. It made them look at their resources, take stock and made them pay attention to what they were actually doing, which they may not otherwise have even noticed. When they start looking at their own schools, to create this internationalization section, they would have to consult with their faculty.... It's not just that you have something appear in a plan. Before it appears is a process which sensitizes the dean to the fact that there are assets there and things that could be done. (personal communication, interview, May 8, 2007)

The incorporation of internationalization into the schools' strategic plans directly addressed this issue by ensuring the relevance of internationalization to prevailing disciplinary concerns. In addition to the customization of internationalization plans by each school, faculty members, likewise, have been given institutional support to develop conferences on their emerging international scholarly interests (Senior administrative leader, personal communication, interview, May 8, 2007). As such, customization is an organizational principle that has enabled faculty at this research university to connect their scholarly, disciplinary agendas with the institution's plans for internationalization.

Coordination

The principle of coordination underscores the significance of a centralized support system for planning, policy development, and information sharing. The principle of coordination, although challenging to develop in a research university with countless international initiatives occurring simultaneously, has been alive in Duke's culture, as indicated by the frequency of interactions of faculty across schools and departments.

According to Merkx, "We've increased the velocity of interaction [of faculty] across units, as a way of helping everybody be more educated and efficient" (personal communication, May 8, 2007).

One of the ways in which Duke has sought to increase the coordination of faculty international activities is through the "International Advisory Committee" (IAC), which is Duke's campus-wide internationalization committee. This committee's charge established by the provost was to provide coordination and exchange of information across schools and international units, such as the international visa office, intercultural programming office, and international and area studies centers (G. W. Merkx, personal communication, interview, August 17, 2007).[12] According to Duke's first internationalization plan (1995), the IAC was to consist of

> Deans from the schools or a faculty member designated by a Dean and an equal number of at-large faculty members appointed by the Provost in consultation with the Deans, the Vice Provost for International Affairs, and other university administrators. The International Affairs Committee will be chaired by the Vice Provost. It [will] work to develop priorities, establish basic policy directions, coordinate activities, identify possible areas of initiative, and provide general advice. (p. 22)

Yet, the committee's power is limited:

> The committee is not a powerful committee. It is an advisory committee.... I think the flow of information is largely among people in the committee and up and down to the administration and from the administration. I think that, probably, it doesn't have a wide influence on faculty [throughout the institution]. (G.W. Merkx, personal communication, interview, August 17, 2007).

Considering its limited power, this study's participants indicated that the IAC serves three overarching functions, albeit primarily for its approximately two dozen faculty and administrative members. These functions include community development, coordination, and information sharing. To illustrate the community development function, Merkx stated,

> In a subtle way, the real function of the committee is to create a sense of community that unites people across campus.... You want to build a community on campus [of] people that care about [internationalization], because they can lobby for things *as a community*. (personal communication, interview, May 8, 2007)

To highlight the coordination function, a senior administrative leader explained that the IAC

> is one of those coordinating hubs.... With an institution as complex as Duke is, with its various facets, you need some place to bring the major players together to talk about what's happening and how to work collaboratively.... So I think the International Affairs Committee is that type of place where you can coordinate and communicate and work collaboratively. (personal communication, interview, May 8, 2007)

To exemplify the information sharing function, Merkx stated,

---

[12] According to Vice Provost Merkx, there is no written charge for Duke's international affairs committee (personal communication, August 17, 2007).

One [of the IAC's roles] is a sharing information function.... This committee shares information [about international activities across schools], so that helps [internation-alization leaders at each school] do their job better and be better prepared. To the extent you do that, of course, you're creating an environment which makes it easier for faculty to do things internationally and not get hung up in red tape and bureaucracy. (personal communication, interview, May 8, 2007)

Despite these coordinating roles, this committee did not emerge as a mechanism for faculty outside the committee to coordinate their international agendas. This perspective was supported by university administrator who articulated,

There are so many [faculty] doing so many different things. The International Affairs Committee is a venue where you come and share this information and try to inform other people, but there is just no way that there is enough time at those meetings where we are truly informed of what everyone else is doing. (personal communication, focus group, May 8, 2007)

Another university administrator echoed, "The International Affairs Committee is not necessarily going to be the place where you find out about [all of the faculty's international activities]" (personal communication, focus group, May 8, 2007). Furthermore, a senior administrative leader advanced understanding of the campus-wide coordination challenges of the IAC through the following comment:

In any place where there is a committee, there is going to be a gap between the committee and the enterprise of individual faculty. [It is critical to make] sure that everybody knows who is on the committee, but also what the functions of the committee are. It's not clear to me what decision making powers and resource allocations the [International Affairs] Committee has. [Faculty] have to know that. (personal communication, interview, May 8, 2007)

Despite the IAC's campus-wide coordination challenges, the coordination prompted by international centers and the international faculty database system provided opportunities for faculty to create synergies among their international endeavors across departments and schools within the university, as well as with neighboring universities. For example, the North Carolina Center for South Asia Studies has promoted the coordination of Duke University faculty interested in South Asia studies with faculty at neighboring universities, including North Carolina Central University, North Carolina State University, and the University of North Carolina-Chapel Hill (Duke University Office of the Vice Provost for International Affairs & Development, 2005e; NC Center for South Asia Studies, 2007).

In addition, an international faculty database system has enabled faculty to search for colleagues engaged in world regions or research topics of interest, so that they can coordinate their scholarly initiatives (Duke

University Office of the Vice Provost for International Affairs & Development, 2005a). This coordinating effort derived, in fact, from Duke's first and second internationalization plans (1995, 2003). In illustration, Duke's first internationalization plan recommended

> immediately beginning a comprehensive inventory of the University's international faculty and research interests, to be compiled as a computer data base and circulated on-line and in hard copy throughout the University and to interested outsiders. Ideally this inventory could be developed and coordinated with similar efforts at neighboring universities, colleges, arts organizations, and research institutions. It will become an invaluable resource enabling faculty…to identify and promptly contact knowledgeable local sources about international matters of specific interest. (p. 15)

Furthermore, Duke's second internationalization plan (2003) reinforced the importance of coordination of international resources for faculty, by advocating for the establishment of an "on-line data base of all [international] agreements that is searchable (e.g., by field or discipline, country, Duke units involved, date of establishment and expiration, principal contact, etc.)" (p. 25). Through Duke's international partnerships and collaborations database (Duke University Office of the Vice Provost for International Affairs & Development, 2005c), faculty can search by country, Duke school, or partner school to find institutions overseas with which Duke has established relationships.

Overall, coordination emerged as an intended, although not pervasive, organizational principle that affected faculty involvement in international scholarship at Duke. In other words, coordination was advocated by Duke's internationalization plans, supported by the IAC for its member faculty only, and promoted by international centers and databases. The limited nature of coordination as an organizational principle and its relation to the next organizational principle—enterpreneurship—will be discussed in a subsequent analysis section.

Entrepreneurship

The principle of entrepreneurship refers to the propensity to seek out, recognize, organize, and implement new initiatives. Entrepreneurship has featured prominently in Duke's "healthy start-up culture" and has encouraged faculty to discover and pursue international initiatives that advance their teaching and research agendas (Senior administrative leader, personal communication, interview, May 8, 2007). Numerous study participants commented on "the entrepreneurial spirit" of Duke's faculty (personal communications, interviews and focus group, May 8, 2007).

Because Duke is not located in a major metropolitan center, the university's geographic location emerged as a catalyst to stimulate faculty entrepreneurship. A university administrator described, "Here at Duke, we are not in Washington, DC. We are not in Boston or San Francisco. We are not on the cutting edge of things international. There are no embassies. This prompts faculty to go out there and find the world" (personal communication, focus group, May 8, 2007). As such, the entrepreneurship of Duke's faculty, aided by the university's geographic location, has propelled faculty to proactively seek out diverse, international perspectives to bring into their classrooms and scholarship.

The nexus of entrepreneurship and faculty involvement in internationalization is, in fact, rooted in Duke's first internationalization plan (1995), which emphasized,

> The University cannot and should not impose an overly centralized, highly structured plan. Its distinguished international reputation to date has been achieved primarily through its faculty, whose research is generally conducted in decentralized, highly entrepreneurial, individual, or team efforts. These independent energies should be fueled. (p. 5)

This philosophy is further supported by the university's current strategic plan (2006), which seeks to "assure continued entrepreneurial initiatives on the part of our schools and institutes while increasing our capability for more centrally coordinated strategic undertakings" (p. 66). As such, entrepreneurship, as an organizational principle that encourages stakeholders to seek out and implement new initiatives, has served as a catalyst for Duke faculty to explore and add new international dimensions to their scholarly work. A discussion of entrepreneurship and its relationship with the organizational principle of coordination will be presented in the cross-case findings and analysis section.

Summary

In sum, five organizational principles emerged as accepted codes of conduct that guided faculty involvement in internationalization. These organizational principles were collaboration, interdisciplinarity, customization, coordination and entrepreneurship. Table 5 provides a synthesis and examples of these principles.

Table 5. Duke's Organizational Principles Used to Develop Faculty Engagement in Internationalization

Organizational principle	Examples
Collaboration	International centers Faculty seminars Overseas medical campus
Interdisciplinarity	International centers Faculty seminars
Customization	Schools' customization of internationalization plans
Coordination	International advisory committee International centers International faculty database system
Entrepreneurship	"Healthy start-up culture" Geographic location

Internationalization Plans

In this section, Duke University's internationalization plan types, internationalization plan roles, and the alignment of faculty engagement strategies articulated in Duke's multiple internationalization plans will be presented.

Internationalization Plan Types

All three internationalization plan types, according to the researcher's internationalization plan typology (as presented in the Appendix), were represented at Duke University. First, Duke has had internationalization incorporated into its previous and current university strategic plans (2001, 2006). Second, Duke has developed two documents explicitly as internationalization plans (1995, 2003). Third, all of Duke's nine schools have incorporated internationalization into their 2006 strategic plans. As such, all three types of internationalization plans indicated in the internationalization plan typology were found at Duke. Implications of the international plan types found at Duke and Richmond will be discussed in a subsequent analysis section.

Internationalization Plan Roles

Data collection and analysis revealed that Duke's internationalization plans served the following roles in increasing faculty engagement in internationalization: (a) increase visibility, (b) create a road map, (c) express intentionality, (d) allocate resources, and (e) customize to disciplinary priorities. In illustration of these internationalization plan roles, a faculty member highlighted,

> [Internationalization plans] are very important because they convey a mission and an aspiration. They are also very important when it comes to internal discussions of resource allocation...., which can migrate from discussions to formal commitments. [The development of an internationalization plan] is a way of educating the board of trustees. It has a lot of very important symbolic, but also resource allocation functions. So I think that [having internationalization plans] is a huge step for us. (personal communication, focus group, May 8, 2007)

A senior administrative leader echoed,

> The [internationalization] plans actually make visible what the aspirations are, what the directions are, what resources [are]. I think [the role of the plans] is fundamental and symbolic.... It makes intentional that the institution is interested and will be supportive of these initiatives. I think that's the signal. (personal communication, interview, May 8, 2007)

To demonstrate the roles served by Duke's institution-wide internationalization plans and school-wide strategic plans that incorporated internationalization, an exchange that took place between two faculty during the focus group is illuminating: A faculty member stated, "The university, of course, has moved forward enormously in formulating its global aspirations and internationalization. But, the execution is at the school level. And, if you think about what deans do, the deans are the vertebrae of the university." Another faculty member added, "The schools are the toes." The first faculty member continued, "Different schools have different reasons to want to internationalize" (personal communications, focus group, May 8, 2007). Given that the execution of internationalization plans occurs "on the ground" at the unit level and each of Duke's schools had distinct rationales and goals for internationalization, it was critical for each school to customize the institutional plans for internationalization to address unique disciplinary priorities.

Internationalization Plan Alignment

The alignment of faculty engagement strategies in Duke's internationalization plans is indicated in Table 6. Each of Duke's internationalization plans, 13 in total, details various strategies to develop faculty engagement in international scholarship. Because all of the faculty engagement strategies were articulated in more than one internationalization plan, the effects of these internationalization plans were multiplied.

Table 6. Alignment of Strategies Articulated in Duke's Internationalization Plans

Strategy	Internationalization plans	
	Number of	Types of
Partnerships w/ overseas institutions	10	USP(1), USP(2), IP(1), IP(2), B, D, Eng, Env, L, M
Funding resources for int'l initiatives	7	USP(1), USP(2), IP(1), IP(2), A, Env, L
International centers	7	USP(1), USP(2), IP(1), B, Env, L
Alignment with university 'Global Health' initiative	6	A, Env, G, L, M, N
Collaborations among departments	5	IP(1), IP(2), Env, L, M
Intentional hiring of faculty w/ int'l expertise	5	USP(2), IP(1), IP(2), D, L
Faculty seminars	4	IP(1), IP(2), A, L
Int'lly focused committees	4	USP(1), IP(1), A, Env
Office of the Vice Provost for Int'l Affairs	4	USP(1), USP(2), IP(1), IP(2)
Support for distinguished int'l visiting scholars	3	IP(1), A, G, L
Int'l conferences	3	IP(1), Eng, Env
Int'l consulting	3	IP(1), Eng, Env
Int'l degree programs	3	B, L, M
Partnerships w/ US institutions	3	IP(1), IP(2), M
Support for faculty/ school interests	3	IP(1), IP(2), N
Technology	3	IP(1), B, G
Int'l faculty scholarship database	2	IP(1), IP(2)
Recommended inclusion of internationalization in tenure and promotion policies	2	IP(1), IP(2)

Note. USP(1)= university strategic plan (2001); USP(2)= university strategic plan (2006); IP(1)=internationalization plan (1995); IP(2)= internationalization plan (2003); A= Arts & Sciences strategic plan (2006); B= Fuqua School of Business strategic plan (2006); D= Divinity School strategic plan (2006); Eng= School of Engineering strategic plan (2006); Env= Nicholas School of the Environment strategic plan (2006); G= Graduate School strategic plan, (2006); L= School of Law strategic plan (2006); M= School of Medicine strategic plan (2006); N= School of Nursing strategic plan (2006).

Specifically, nine faculty engagement strategies were incorporated in two different types of internationalization plans, including university strategic plans, distinct internationalization plans, or school strategic plans. These strategies were collaboration among departments, faculty seminars, development of the Office of the Vice Provost for International Affairs, development of or participation in international conferences, international consulting, US partnerships, support for faculty and school interests, use of technology, and development and use of an international faculty scholarship database. What is more, four strategies were emphasized in all three types of internationalization plans. These strategies included partnerships with overseas institutions, funding resources for international initiatives, intentional hiring of faculty with international expertise, and participation in internationally focused committees. As support and reinforcement was given at multiple institutional levels, the alignment of strategies to engage faculty in international activities supported the operationalization of Duke's internationalization plans.

Duke University Case Study Summary

In summary, this section presented the story of Duke University's development of faculty engagement in internationalization. The findings discussed emerged from the interviews, focus groups, and documentation conducted for this study. Table 7 provides a synthesis of the academic activities, organizational practices, and organizational principles that supported faculty engagement in Duke's internationalization.

Table 7. Synthesis of Duke's Strategies Used to Develop Faculty Engagement in Internationalization

Academic activities	Organizational practices	Organizational principles
Faculty seminars International degree programs Development of an overseas medical campus	Substantial investments in internationalization Strategic use of electronic resources Development of international centers Reaccreditation self-study	Collaboration Interdisciplinarity Customization Coordination Entrepreneurship

Moreover, all three types of internationalization plans, according to the researcher's internationalization plan typology, were found at Duke, including university strategic plans, distinct documents, and unit plans. The four overarching roles these plans served in developing faculty engagement in Duke's internationalization were to (a) increase visibility, (b) create a road map, (c) express intentionality, (d) allocate resources, and (e) customize internationalization to disciplinary priorities. Finally, there was the strong alignment between the faculty engagement strategies articulated in Duke's various internationalization plans, which promoted faculty involvement in international activities at multiple institutional levels. Implications of these findings will be discussed in a subsequent section on cross-case analysis.

Case Study of University of Richmond

This section presents data collected on strategies used for engaging faculty in the operationalization of internationalization plans at the University of Richmond. The main research question that framed the data collection and analysis was as follows: How has the development of faculty engagement affected the operationalization of internationalization plans This main research question is operationalized through five subtopics, which examine the (a) context, (b) academic activities, (c) organizational practices, (d) organizational principles, and (e) types and alignment of internationalization plans that have affected faculty engagement in internationalization. This section is organized by these subtopics.

Context

Background information about the context in which faculty engaged in the operationalization of internationalization plans at the University of Richmond opens this section. This information includes the university's founding, school composition, and demographics. Next, the historical development of faculty engagement in internationalization plans at Richmond will be explained briefly. Finally, the section will conclude with a summary of the contextual findings that affected faculty involvement in Richmond's internationalization plans.

Background

Located on 350 acres of woodlands and a lake in Virginia's capital city, the University of Richmond was founded in 1830 when Virginia Baptists opened a seminary for men (University of Richmond, 2007a, 2007b). Shortly thereafter, seminary leaders added a literary studies program, which led to the incorporation of Richmond College in 1840 (University of Richmond, 2007b). In 1866, after the Civil War left Richmond College virtually bankrupt, James Thomas, a leading tobacconist in the Richmond area, donated $5,000, a major gift at the time, to revitalize the college (University of Richmond, 2007b).

A private baccalaureate college, the University of Richmond is comprised of five schools. The University first opened the T.C. Williams School of Law in 1870. Westhampton College, a college designed specifically for women, was founded in 1914, shortly after which the Graduate School of Arts and Sciences opened in 1921 (Carnegie Foundation for the Advancement of Teaching, 2006b; University of Richmond, 2007b). These two colleges were later combined when the School of Arts & Sciences was formed in 1990. After the E. Claiborne Robins School of Business was established in 1949, its namesake, E. Claiborne Robins, who was a trustee and alumnus, donated $50 million in 1969—the largest gift made to a higher education institution at the time (University of Richmond, 2007b). In 1962, the opening of the School of Continuing Studies fortified Richmond's connections with the surrounding community (University of Richmond, 2007d). In 1987, a gift of $20 million by alumnus Robert S. Jepson led to the founding of the Jepson School of Leadership Studies, which was the first school of its kind in the US (University of Richmond, 2007b). With its continued developments, the University of Richmond's endowment totaled approximately $1.6 billion at the end of the 2006-2007 academic year—the 43rd largest higher education institutional endowment in the US (National Association of College and University Business Officers, 2007; University of Richmond Advancement, 2007). Descriptive and demographic information about the university is provided in Table 8.

Moreover, the University of Richmond has received national recognition for its effective internationalization practices. For example, Richmond was spotlighted in NAFSA: Association of International Educator's (2006c) "Internationalizing the Campus: Profiles of Success at Colleges and Universities" report and received an honorable mention in the Institute for International Education's (2002) "Andrew Heiskell Awards for Innovation in International Education." The University of Richmond was also recognized in Newsweek's 2008 college guide as the "hottest for international studies" (Matthews, 2007, p. 58). Thus, with national recognition for internationalization, a large endowment, a substantial percentage of students who study abroad, and two different types of internationalization plans, the University of Richmond has been well poised to engage its faculty in internationalization.

Table 8. Descriptive and Demographic Information about University of
 Richmond

Institutional Characteristics of the University of Richmond	
Year founded	1830
Location	Richmond, VA
Geographic size	350 acres
Schools	Arts & Sciences Business Continuing Studies Leadership Studies Law
Institutional type	Private, baccalaureate college
Endowment	$1.6 billion
National ranking of endowment	43rd
Undergraduate students	2,857
Undergraduate students who are foreign nationals	6%
Graduate and professional students	697
Graduate students who are foreign nationals	4%
Students who study abroad	70%
Tenured or tenure-track faculty	242
Regular-rank faculty	140
Faculty who are foreign nationals	7%

Note. Data were derived from "Carnegie Classifications," by the Carnegie Foundation for the Advancement of Teaching; "Fast Facts," by University of Richmond, 2007; and "2006 NACUBO Endowment Study," by National Association of College and University Business Officers, 2007.

Historical Context for Faculty Engagement in Richmond's Internationalization Plans

In order to examine the strategies used to develop faculty engagement in Richmond's internationalization plans, it is important to understand the historical context in which this engagement has taken place. In the early 1980s, after discussing the concept of "international competence" at an academic deans' conference, Richmond's dean of arts and sciences pulled together a committee of faculty from various disciplines to discuss the topic of "international competence" (Faculty member, personal communication, focus group, May 3, 2007; University of Richmond Ad Hoc Committee on International Studies, 1986). The arts and sciences dean asked this ad hoc committee on international studies "to figure out what that is and whether we have enough of it and if we don't, what we can do about that" (Faculty member, personal communication, focus group, May 3, 2007). As Louis Tremaine (1994), current chair of the English department and member of this ad hoc committee on international studies wrote in a book chapter on the internationalization of Richmond's curriculum,

> The particular charge given this committee, as it turns out, was important in determining the direction we have traveled since. We were not asked in this committee to create an international studies program (though we subsequently did), or to establish a series of area studies programs. We were not, in fact, asked to create anything at all. Rather, our charge was to study several related questions:
>
> - What is international competence?
> - Can undergraduates acquire it as part of their college training and experience?
> - If so, are our undergraduates acquiring it?
> - If they are not, what might our university be capable of doing to help them acquire it? (p. 276)

This committee convened 16 times between December 1983 and March 1986 to consider the overall status of international education at the university, discuss these questions, and make recommendations for improvement (University of Richmond Ad Hoc Committee on International Studies, 1986).

After two and a half years of assessing the broad context for international education in the US, including national surveys and studies, and the specific context of international education at the University of Richmond, the committee developed Richmond's first internationalization plan, "Enhancing 'International Competence' at the University of Richmond" (University of Richmond Ad Hoc Committee on International Studies, 1986). The committee determined that international competence is the ability to relate knowledge about global events and relationships to one's own life and work.

However, the plan noted the following challenge to the development of international competence at Richmond: "Despite the growing interest of both faculty and students in various forms of international study, the University's system of support for such activities is fragmented and relatively limited" (p. 7). Accordingly, the plan highlighted the following goals:

> [provide] systematic oversight of programs in international education, [develop a] coherent curriculum in international studies.... [and] convey a sense of institutional

conviction that international education is a central component of a liberal (and even pre-professional) education. (pp. 11-12)

To realize these goals, the plan offered the following overarching recommendations: (a) consolidate the university's international activities and programs under one roof in an Office of International Education administered by a director and overseen by a faculty committee and (b) create an international studies degree program which would offer an opportunity for coherent study of international issues through an interdisciplinary curriculum (University of Richmond Ad Hoc Committee on International Studies, 1986).

Because the plan advocated that "the planning and oversight of the curriculum in particular would require close cooperation and consultation with faculty" (p. 14), the following recommendations were outlined: The Office of International Education should

1. Work with departments and deans in developing and sponsoring University of Richmond programs abroad;

2. Encourage faculty and course development in international studies

3. Work with a faculty in developing and administering the international studies degree program;

4. Be led by a director with strong academic credentials, including a terminal degree in an appropriate field of study;

5. Develop a campus-wide international education committee for faculty to provide guidance on the continuing development of "international competence" at Richmond. (University of Richmond Ad Hoc Committee on International Studies, 1986)

Overall, Richmond's first internationalization plan sought to provide centralization and, thereby, coordination of international initiatives throughout the institution in order to establish a foundation from which "international competence" could be developed.

A year after the internationalization plan was institutionalized, a strategy to develop faculty engagement in internationalization was formalized. Through funding received from Richmond's development office, the new Office of International Education faculty director created the first "Faculty Abroad Seminar," a biennial program through which an interdisciplinary group of faculty travel to countries infrequently visited by Americans, engage in discussions with academic counterparts and government officials, and gain new international knowledge and experiences, which they incorporate into their teaching and research (U. F. Gabara, personal communication, interview, May 3, 2007; University of Richmond Office of International

Education, 2007c). The faculty abroad seminars will be discussed in detail in the subsequent section on academic activities.

In 2000 and again in 2004, updated institutional goals for internationalization were provided by the university's strategic plan and revised mission statement. In particular, the university's strategic plan highlighted the importance of integrating cross-cultural and international perspectives into teaching and research at Richmond (University of Richmond, 2000). Moreover, foundational support for internationalization was advanced when the faculty approved Richmond's mission statement to include the preparation of students for "responsible leadership in a global and pluralistic society" (University of Richmond, 2004, para. 1). Although the university plan and revised mission statement laid out updated, overarching goals for internationalization, they did not provide action steps through which to realize those goals.

In order to raise funds from potential donors and allocate internal resources, Richmond's provost advocated the necessity to develop a road map for the operationalization of those goals (Senior administrative leader, personal communication, interview, May 3, 2007). As such, the development of Richmond's second internationalization plan began in 2004, when the provost called for the creation of a plan to crystallize the momentum, develop a long-term vision, and specific actions to realize that vision for Richmond's internationalization (Senior administrative leader, personal communication, interview, May 3, 2007; University of Richmond, 2006). The rationale for the development of this internationalization plan was articulated in the document as follows:

> Internationalization of education and co-curricular activities is one of the central values at the University of Richmond. We have created a community of students, staff, and faculty in which cross-cultural and international knowledge, attitudes, experiences and action are part of the present and a heritage for the future. Our mission is to help students develop a world view, see and analyze issues from various perspectives, understand the broad range of human experience and celebrate the diversity of the human spirit. International education is already in many ways integrated into the fabric of this institution. (University of Richmond International Education Committee, 2006c, p. 1)

In order to address this mission, an internationalization plan committee, which included faculty, administrators, trustees, and students, was created (University of Richmond International Education Committee, 2006c). The committee was organized into subcommittees to examine in depth the resources, people, and programs necessary to advance Richmond's internationalization.

This request from the provost set in motion a year of meetings, through which the taskforce created a mission and vision of internationalization, "SWOT" analysis of its strengths, weaknesses, opportunities, and threats, and internationalization goals and objectives (University of Richmond International Education Committee, 2006c). The synthesis of this information resulted in Richmond's "Strategic Plan for International Education" (2006), which was approved by the president and provost. This plan included updated goals and recommendations for internationalization: In particular the plan articulated the following goal:

> to promote international education as a core value of the University and to integrate internationalization fully into current and future strategic institutional objectives and initiatives, and thus to move the University to the next level of internationalization – the American Council on Education's "highly active institution" category. (University of Richmond International Education Committee, 2006c, p. 1)

To operationalize this goal, the plan offered particular recommendations and action steps relating to faculty engagement (see Table 9).

Table 9. Recommendations and Action Steps Advocated in Richmond's 2006 Internationalization Plan

Recommendations	Action Steps
Create an International Living and Learning Center on campus to bring together the expanding array of international programs	Engage faculty in a process to define the specific aims and functions of the Center
Expand and strengthen the international outlook of the university community, and further internationalize the curricula and programs in each of the University's schools	Continue the Faculty Seminar Abroad biennially as a proven way to broaden the international perspectives of faculty Promote recognition of international work (research, teaching, and service) in hiring, tenure, promotion, and merit pay increases Continue funding in support of the development of new courses with significant international content

As such, the goals, recommendations, and action steps provided by this plan created a road map through which to advance Richmond's internationalization. Overall, the extent to which Richmond has formalized its commitments to internationalization has provided significant visibility and support for faculty to engage in internationalization.

Unanticipated Factors

Although numerous factors that affected faculty involvement in Richmond's internationalization were expected due to the extensive literature review conducted for this study, the influence of students on faculty engagement in internationalization was unanticipated, as this factor had not been revealed in previous studies.

In fact, faculty from diverse disciplines indicated that students' inquires about international perspectives prompted them to address international and cross-cultural issues in their teaching, curricular developments, and research. For example, a faculty member acknowledged that a discussion with a student led to their collaboration on the development of a new course that included a study abroad component in Austria (University of Richmond International Education Committee, 2006b). In addition, because 70% of Richmond students study abroad, faculty have frequently (a) engaged in conversations on international topics with students, (b) wrote recommendations to advocate for their students to study abroad, and (c) discussed their students' study abroad opportunities with colleagues (U. F. Gabara, personal communication, interview, May 3, 2007). What is more, return study abroad students have served as links for Richmond faculty to establish research partnerships with faculty at the institutions abroad where students have studied (U. F. Gabara, personal communication, interview, May 3, 2007).

Academic Activities

At the University of Richmond, academic activities encouraged faculty engagement in internationalization, by providing opportunities for faculty to add international perspectives to their teaching and research. Such academic activities included the development of the faculty seminar abroad program and international teaching opportunities.

Faculty Seminar Abroad

The development of Richmond's unique faculty seminar abroad program emerged as one of the most significant strategies used to develop faculty engagement in internationalization at the University of Richmond. Through this biennial seminar, which has been recognized as an exemplary practice by the Institute of International Education (2002) and NAFSA: Association of International Educators (2006c), has taken place 14 times since its inauguration in 1989. During the seminar, a group of eight to 12 faculty travel for three weeks during the summer to countries infrequently visited by Americans (Gabara, 1994; University of Richmond Communications, 2006; University of Richmond Office of International Education, 2007c).

The seminar was established in 1988 when the Office of International Education's new faculty director, Uliana Gabara, received discretionary funds from the Office of Development. In order to develop students' international competence, Gabara believed that it was first necessary to enhance faculty members' international expertise and experiences. Gabara explained, "It became clear that if one wanted to approach internationalization broadly across the disciplines, what we needed to do was start with the faculty" (University of Richmond Communications, 2006, para. 4). Thus, out of this contention and the funds received from the Office of Development, the faculty seminar abroad emerged as a strategy through which Richmond faculty have honed their skills and knowledge to take part in their institution's internationalization.

The seminar itself is embedded with several strategies to engage faculty in internationalization, which include the (a) application process, (b) faculty participant-led predeparture workshops, (c) extensive travel and wide ranging discussions abroad, and (d) postseminar report of learning outcomes and plans for curricular integration.

Application process. The seminar begins with an application process, which asks faculty to consider (a) how their participation in the seminar will contribute to their teaching and research, (b) their readiness to devote time to predeparture meetings, readings, participant led disciplinary presentations, and discussions with regional experts, (c) willingness to write a report of the seminar outcomes and plans for integration into teaching, (d) future use of contacts developed abroad through seminar, and (g) interest in interdisciplinary research and teaching (University of Richmond Office of International Education, 2007d). This application process prompts faculty to engage in a thought process about the potential connections of this seminar to their professional agendas, the time necessary to invest before, during, and after the seminar to maximize those connections, and possible opportunities to integrate what they will learn in the seminar process into their teaching and research. Thus, faculty are actively involved in linking the seminar to their scholarly agendas from step one in the seminar—the application process.

Faculty participant-led predeparture workshops. The predeparture meetings take in the form of a "mutual teaching exercise" (Kelleher, 1996, p. 322). Through the series of six to 10 predeparture meetings, faculty participants make presentations on the region to be visited from their disciplinary perspectives, suggest speakers, jointly construct a reading list, establish a reference section in the library with relevant sources, discuss texts selected by the group, and engage in discussions with regional experts (Gabara, 2006; University of Richmond Office of International Education, 2005c). In illustration of the benefits of the predeparture preparation process, a senior administrative leader described that through these meetings and readings, faculty "[study] the culture and the country and the customs before they even go, so that they will be equipped to deal effectively and to learn as much as possible" (personal communication, interview, May 3, 2007). Thus, participants are actively involved in their seminar preparation process. Because faculty proactively develop a knowledge base of various disciplinary perspectives on regional issues in advance of the seminar, they enable themselves to maximize their learning opportunities during the seminar abroad.

Extensive travel and wide-ranging discussions abroad. During the three weeks abroad on the seminar, participants travel extensively and engage in wide-ranging discussions with academic counterparts, government officials, business people, journalists, grass root activists, and others, so that they can "get the pulse of the place" (Gabara, 2006, p. 2). Importantly, while faculty study and experience the aesthetic, economic, political, religious, and social culture of the region abroad, they also share field experiences with their interdisciplinary group of colleagues (Gabara, 1994, 2006). As a senior administrative leader pointed out, "Simply spending that time with each other as roommates and travel companions stimulates the conversation about internationalization among those faculty" (personal communication, interview, May 3, 2007). Thus, by providing faculty with opportunities to experience and discuss new cultural revelations with colleagues from various disciplinary vantage points, the seminar provides support for faculty to draw connections about newly acquired cultural knowledge to their scholarly agendas and their institution's internationalization plans.

Postseminar report of learning outcomes and plans for curricular integration. Upon return to campus after the seminar, participants are required to write a report of what they have learned through the seminar and their plans for incorporating those lessons and perspectives into their teaching and research (Gabara, 1994, 2006; University of Richmond Office of International Education, 2005a). These reports are illuminating of the skills and knowledge faculty developed through the seminars and their plans for integrating international perspectives into their teaching and research (University of Richmond Office of International Education, 2005a).

Seminar outcomes relating to faculty engagement in internationalization. According to faculty postseminar reports, interviews, and the focus group conducted for this study, the success of the seminar as a strategy to develop faculty engagement in internationalization is indicated by the following outcomes: the development of (a) transformational experiences, (b) interdisciplinary networks and collaborations, (c) internationalization of curricula, (d) international research projects, (e) increased disciplinary knowledge, and (f) increased awareness of and access to international opportunities. As the first two outcomes emerged through all types of data collection methods (i.e., interviews, focus group, and documentation) and all types of participants (i.e., AIEA representative, senior administrative leaders, and faculty members), these two outcomes will be explained subsequently.

The seminar has produced a "transformational experience" for participants. Numerous faculty explained that although they had been non-travelers prior to the seminar, the seminar changed their vision of what is possible in their teaching, research, and personal life. This transformational effect is illuminated through the following comments:

"Faculty members are often transformed by the experience and students hear about it for years." (Gabara, 1994, p. 158)

"For some faculty, it is a life-changing experience." (Faculty member, personal communication, focus group, May 3, 2007)

"It can take someone who is pretty homebound and can get them really interested and excited [in other countries]. And, if you get them voluntarily interested and excited, that is best." (Faculty member, personal communication, focus group, May 3, 2007)

"I went [on the seminar] to India and that was really a life changing experience. And faculty can bring those things back." (Senior administrative leader, personal communication, interview, May 3, 2007)

In addition, after the seminar to Ghana and Senegal in 1992, one faculty member communicated the overarching lesson he learned by using the Ghanaian proverb, "Hunt in every forest, for there is wisdom and good hunting in them all" (Kelleher, 1996, p. 324). Another faculty member reflected, "When everything is so different, strange, and new, the sense of being alive is profound" (Kelleher, 1996, p. 324). After the seminar to Turkey and Cyprus in 2005, a faculty member explained that the seminar prompted participants to "use their telescopes, microscopes, and kaleidoscopes as well as their cameras to understand Turkey" (University of Richmond Office of International Education, 2005a).

An unanticipated outcome emerged from the multidisciplinary group selected for each seminar: Through the group of seminar alumni, a faculty support network for internationalization across campus has been established. This network reaches broadly and deeply throughout the institution, as the seminar alumni group is comprised of more than one third of Richmond's faculty, including faculty from 24 departments who collectively have visited 28 countries through the seminar (University of Richmond Office of International Education, 2007f). In fact, numerous participants in this study explained that the seminar encouraged dialogue among faculty from a variety of disciplines, as illustrated by the following comments:

> "People talk about the silos, both academic and personal silos, and this [seminar] tends to break down some of those separations." (U. F. Gabara, personal communication, interview, May 3, 2007)

> "[The seminar] can help build bridges across schools. I went to southeast Asia with the group [that] had two psychologists, a journalist, an economist, two people from business [among others]." (Faculty member, personal communication, focus group, May 3, 2007)

> "As a result of the faculty [from various disciplines] spending time together on the seminar, through conversations for the month they are traveling and discovering new cultures together, there is a basis for collaboration they haven't realized before." (Senior administrative leader, interview, May 3, 2007)

Furthermore, as a result of the seminars, interdisciplinary and international faculty collaborations have flourished. As an example, Gabara explained, "Two faculty members, a philosopher and a theater specialist, have jointly developed a course, which they are teaching together. They have done it now two or three times" (personal communication, interview, May 3, 2007). Moreover, according to postseminar faculty reports, this dialogue has led to many more interdisciplinary collaborations in international teaching and research, such as teaching collaborations between classicists and literary scholars and research collaborations between political scientists and economists (University of Richmond Office of International Education, 2007e).

Summary. Due to the multiple initiatives to develop faculty engagement embedded within the seminar and its meaningful outcomes, the faculty seminar abroad has served as an important strategy to develop faculty engagement in internationalization at the University of Richmond.

International Teaching Opportunities

Despite the prominence of the faculty seminar abroad, international teaching opportunities also served as avenues through which faculty engaged in Richmond's internationalization. Three types of teaching opportunities emerged, which include (a) leading and teaching on summer study abroad programs, (b) integrating study abroad components into courses, and (c) teaching in the international studies program.

Leading and teaching on summer study abroad programs. For many years Richmond faculty have received support to lead and teach on study abroad programs (Gabara, 2007; University of Richmond Office of International Education, 2007h). For example, recently a history professor led a summer study abroad program at Cambridge University to focus on the background, causes, and outbreak of World War I and a geography professor conducted a summer study abroad program to Jamaica and Guyana to focus on Caribbean geography and sustainable development (University of Richmond International Education Committee, 2006b, 2007a). In addition, Richmond's international education committee recently approved the development of new faculty-led summer study abroad programs in Mexico and Italy and the extension of a faculty-led program in Chile and Easter Island (University of Richmond International Education Committee, 2007a). The type of support faculty have received to conduct these programs will be addressed in the section of this chapter on organizational practices, in the subsection on substantial investments in internationalization.

Integrating study abroad components into on-campus courses. In the last few years, Richmond faculty have received support to add a one- or two-week overseas study component to an otherwise on-campus course (Gabara, 2007; University of Richmond Office of International Education, 2007h). For example, in 2007, two English professors led a semester-long research seminar that incorporated a two week excursion to Shanghai to conduct field research and a music professor incorporated a study and performance component in Spain into an otherwise on campus-based course (University of Richmond International Education Committee, 2007a; University of Richmond Office of International Education, 2006). Again, the type of support faculty have received to conduct these programs will be addressed in the organizational practices section of this chapter. All in all, manifold opportunities to lead and teach on summer study abroad programs presented faculty with mechanisms to engage in teaching overseas.

International studies major. Not only was the international studies major proposed by an interdisciplinary group of faculty through the 1986 internation-alization plan, but it continues to serve as a means for faculty from diverse disciplines to engage in international scholarship (University of Richmond, 2007c). Faculty firmly expressed that a series of disparate area studies programs would not serve to promote campus-wide faculty engagement in internationalization at Richmond. Rather through the purposeful creation of a singular international studies program, "a common enterprise" was established through which faculty, such as those from the economics, geography, history, political science, and sociology departments, have participated in internationally focused teaching and research (Faculty member, personal communication, focus group, May 3, 2007). The following comment highlights the importance of this centralization of faculty focus on international studies:

> After a lot of conversation, the committee on international studies made a very conscious decision to establish a major in international studies, not in African studies, nation studies, Latin American studies, and so on. They would all be out there operating as separate enterprises.... [The centralized international studies program] meant that the faculty was working together. It simply brought faculty together from various disciplines and various area studies to work together.... So there is a lot of critical mass there and, therefore, a sense of substance and heft to the program that adds to that kind of momentum. (Faculty member, focus group, personal communication, focus group, May 3, 2007)

As this statement exemplifies, the international studies program has provided infrastructural support for faculty to create connections among their various international interests and disciplinary perspectives. Through intentionally creating a centralized international academic program rather than decentralized area studies program, Richmond has created a strong structural foundation from which faculty explore international dimensions of their disciplines in the classroom.

Table 10. Richmond's Academic Activities Used to Develop Faculty
Engagement in Internationalization

General strategy	Examples of specific strategies
Faculty seminar abroad	Application process Faculty participant-led predeparture workshops Extensive travel and wide-ranging discussions abroad Postseminar report of learning outcomes and curricular integration plans
International teaching opportunities	Leading and teaching on summer study abroad programs Integrating study abroad components into courses Teaching in international studies program

Summary

In sum, two overarching types of academic activities were used at the University of Richmond to develop faculty engagement in internationalization. Table 10 details these academic activities, which include the faculty seminar abroad and international teaching opportunities.

Organizational Practices

Organizational practices refer to the policies, structures, and actions usually initiated by senior administrative leaders that affect faculty work. At the University of Richmond, organizational practices encouraged faculty engagement in internationalization, by providing critical infrastructure, incentives, and communication mechanisms to support faculty in developing international dimensions in their teaching and research. Such organizational practices included Richmond's substantial investments in internationalization and development of the Office of International Education. However, the lack of inclusion of internationalization in Richmond's tenure and promotion policies emerged as an obstacle that hindered the engagement of some faculty in international scholarship. These organizational practices will be discussed in turn.

Substantial Investments in Internationalization

Richmond has made substantial financial investments to support faculty engagement in international initiatives. These include (a) "Quest International" faculty programming and course development grants, (b) curriculum internationalization grants, (c) Weinstein summer international project grants, (d) and School of Arts & Sciences overseas conferences travel grants. As the first three grant programs emerged as particularly significant sources of funding for faculty to participate in international scholarship, they will be addressed in further detail.

Quest International faculty programming and course development grants. The university's signature program, "The Richmond Quest," which was launched by the president in 2000, has provided significant funding for faculty to internationalize their courses and research (University of Richmond, 2007b). The Richmond Quest is a unique program through which, for periods of two years, faculty, students, and administrators collectively have explored a single pervasive question, submitted by a student (University of Richmond, 2007b). Through its parallel program, "Quest International," faculty have been supported to create internationally focused courses and research projects related to the current Quest theme (University of Richmond,

2007h). Specifically, "Quest International" has offered faculty (a) programming grants, of up to approximately $10,000, to support internationally focused research, curricular, and co-curricular endeavors, (b) course development grants, of up to $3,500, to support the creation of new internationally focused courses, and (c) course revision grants, of up to $1,500, to support the integration of international components into existing courses (University of Richmond, 2007e, 2007f, 2007g). For example, in 2004, Quest grants enabled two English department faculty to take ten students to Bombay, India to conduct research for a study on "Negotiating Change: Twenty-First Century Indian Identity in Mumbai" (University of Richmond International Education Committee, 2004). As such, the Quest program has served as an innovative mechanism through which Richmond faculty have been supported to integrate international components into their teaching and research.

Curriculum internationalization grants. Distinct from the Quest program, curriculum internationalization grants have encouraged faculty to develop new courses with significant international content and to substantially infuse international perspectives into existing courses. Faculty applications to this grant program, which is funded through Office of International Education discretionary funds, have increased by 40% since the program's inception in 2003 (University of Richmond International Education Committee, 2004, 2007b). Awards of $3,000 to $3,500 for the development of new courses and $1,500 to $2,000 for revised courses have been granted to faculty as incentives to internationalize their curricula (University of Richmond Office of International Education, 2007b). In illustration of the effect of curriculum internationalization grants, in 2006, a law school professor received a curriculum internationalization grant to create an international intellectual property course and a psychology professor received a grant to create a cross-cultural psychopathology course (University of Richmond Office of International Education, 2007b). Although awards were granted to only 17% of the faculty who submitted grant applications in 2007, this funding program has promoted widespread faculty engagement in internationalization, as all applicants have developed foundations for internationalizing their courses through the grant application process (U. F. Gabara, personal communication, interview, May 3, 2007; University of Richmond International Education Committee, 2007b).

Weinstein grants for summer international projects. Through the summer international project grants funded by Richmond alumna and former trustee, Carole Weinstein, a longtime advocate of internationalization, faculty have been prompted to engage in innovative, international teaching, research, and service endeavors (Gabara, 2005; University of Richmond Communications, 2003; University of Richmond Office of International Education, 2007a). For example, in 2006, a faculty member received funding to work with women and children from the Mixtecan, southwestern region of Mexico who reside in the Richmond community (University of Richmond International Education Committee, 2006a; University of Richmond Office of International Education, 2007a). Like the curriculum internationalization grant program, faculty interest in the Weinstein international grants has continued to rise. In fact, from 2006 to 2007, faculty applications to this grant program increased by 20% (University of Richmond International Education Committee, 2007b). Thus, the Weinstein summer international grant program has served as a mechanism through which faculty are provided with financial resources to explore international dimensions in their scholarship and service.

Development of Office of International Education

The centralization of Richmond's internationalization initiatives in a single office led by a well-respected faculty member has provided leadership for the development of financial, programmatic, and human resources that have stimulated and supported campus-wide faculty involvement in international activities. The breadth and depth of the impact of Richmond's Office of International Education (OIE) has been supported by the institution's size and type, as it is a medium-sized, baccalaureate college (Carnegie Foundation for the Advancement of Teaching, 2006b).

Academic standing of international education leader. In addition to these institutional characteristics, the OIE's strong impact on faculty engagement in internationalization has been made possible by its dean, who holds the Carole M. Weinstein Chair of International Education, as of 2003 (University of Richmond Communications, 2003). The importance of the academic standing of Richmond's international education leader has its roots in Richmond's 1986 internationalization plan, which advocated that Richmond's international education leader "should have appropriate academic credentials, including a terminal degree in an appropriate field of study" (p. 14). In 2007, numerous faculty and administrators cited that the OIE's leader's academic standing gave the office and its internationalization initiatives invaluable credibility, which, in turn, prompted faculty engagement. For example, a senior administrative leader reflected, "I think it is also important, very critical, that the leader have academic credentials herself. Dr. Gabara has a Ph.D. She has credibility with the faculty because of her own area of study, expertise, and accomplishments" (personal communication, interview, May 3, 2007). Another university administrator concurred: "I do think that the fact that the person who has held this position has had faculty status...has a lot to do with the [faculty] support for internationalization that has evolved" (personal communication, focus group, May 3, 2007). A faculty member added, "She is an extremely well educated person, extremely bright, astute, and intellectually active and engaged person.... She certainly does have the respect of the faculty" (personal communication, interview, August 3, 2007). As such, the intellectual engagement of Richmond's international education leader has contributed to the development of widespread faculty involvement in the university's internationalization plans.

Strategic use of electronic resources. The OIE's strategic use of electronic resources has enabled faculty to become aware of opportunities to engage in international teaching, research, and service. First, the OIE Web site has served as a portal through which faculty have accessed information about international opportunities. For example, through the faculty section of OIE's Web site faculty have had access to (a) examples of internationalized syllabi, (b) faculty traveling abroad forms, (c) hiring foreign faculty information, (d) visiting overseas partner institutions guidelines, (e) academic travel to Cuba information, and (f) taking students abroad guidelines and checklists (University of Richmond Office of International Education, 2007b). Second, not only has OIE's Web site served as a gateway for faculty to access information about international opportunities, but it has served as a forum through which OIE has collected information about faculty members' international expertise and interests, such as through the "International Education Faculty Survey" (University of Richmond Office of International Education, 2007g).

Third, the strategic e-mails sent out by the OIE dean at the beginning of each semester increase faculty awareness of the number and countries of international students who will be in their classes, the number of students who will not be in their classes since they are studying abroad, and strategies for integrating international students' perspectives into classroom discussions. Gabara explained,

> Publicizing statistics [to faculty] is very, very important. At the beginning of every semester, I send out to all the faculty a note saying, "This semester you will have in your classes 100 students returning from study abroad with new knowledge and new interests. I hope you will give them a voice. This semester 250 students will not be in your classes because they are abroad in so many countries doing so and so. This semester in your classes you will have students from 70 countries—I'm sure their contributions to every issue you are teaching about can be different from other students. I hope you will elicit their different points of view." (personal communication, interview, May 3, 2007)

In illustration of the importance of the OIE dean's strategic e-mails, numerous participants commented that they and their colleagues have gained insights into how to integrate international students into their classes and gained awareness of international professional development opportunities through these e-mails. For example, a faculty member reflected,

> What do you do with [international students] when they are in your classroom? I find that to be a problematic question, because you want to draw upon their different experiences and their perspectives, but you don't want to single them out and make them feel like they have to represent an entire culture. So, often, Uliana will send us e-mails and urge us to take advantage of our international students and their experiences (personal communication, interview, May 3, 2007).

A senior administrative leader further described what makes the OIE dean's e-mails effective in stimulating faculty engagement: "There is a systematic way that she has of promoting by notices and announcements of the activities and workshops to draw the faculty into the whole experience of educating students and participating in [internationalization]" (personal communication, interview, May 3, 2007). Thus, the strategic use of electronic resources has enabled faculty throughout the university to become informed about how to engage in their institution's internationalization plans.

Dramatic gestures and iconic moments. "Dramatic gestures" and "iconic moments" have stimulated faculty to engage in the internationalization of Richmond. These powerful, symbolic organizational practices include the faculty seminar abroad, the OIE's reimbursement of passport fees for faculty, and the annual international faculty award. First, numerous faculty and administrators interviewed described the faculty seminar abroad as a "dramatic" experience, which not only stimulated their involvement in international activities in their personal and professional lives, but also signaled to the university community and beyond that Richmond values, supports, and is focused on the development of international education (personal communications, interviews and focus group, May 3, 2007). Second, OIE's announcement that it would cover faculty's passport fees prompted an "iconic moment," which yet again signaled to faculty that the university supports teaching and research overseas through rhetoric as well as resources (U. F. Gabara, personal communication, interview, May 3, 2007). Gabara described her decision to cover faculty member's passport fees as follows: "I wanted to give a signal that everybody ought to have one and always be ready to go [overseas]. It is a very dramatic gesture, and yet not a very expensive one" (personal communication, interview, May 3, 2007). Third, the annual international faculty award, which is given by the Office of International Education at a festive dinner dance with faculty, administrators, students and spotlighted in numerous university publications, makes visible to the entire university community that faculty engagement in internationalization is valued and rewarded. In illustration of the importance of dramatic gestures and iconic moments, Gabara explained,

> A lot of these [strategies to engage faculty in internationalization] should be dramatic gestures. So that you get kind of an iconic moment, you do symbolic gestures. You have to be visible, and sometimes the drama is greater than the substance. The drama plays a very important role in all of these endeavors, especially in the kind of majority culture that we live in where everything is hyped. You have to do some hyping in order to make it very visible. (personal communication, interview, May 3, 2007)

As this comment highlights, dramatic gestures and iconic moments have served as catalysts for faculty to commence or reinvigorate their involvement in their universities' internationalization.

Lack of inclusion of internationalization in tenure and promotion policies. The lack of an explicit inclusion of international scholarship in Richmond's tenure and promotion policies emerged as an organizational practice that hindered the involvement of some faculty in international initiatives. However, two divergent perspectives emerged on this issue. Some faculty and administrators expressed that without the incorporation of internationalization into the tenure and promotion policies disincentives exist for faculty to focus attention on integrating international perspectives into their teaching and research. This perspective is illuminated through the following statements:

> The tenure and promotion system is a brutal one in terms of what is going to count to allow you to get tenure, so there are some disincentives to being adventurous. (Faculty member, personal communication, interview, May 3, 2007)

> Junior faculty especially feel that they must not pick up their head from the research [and] they must not go away because they can be misconstrued. (U. F. Gabara, personal communication, interview, May 3, 2007)

From an alternate vantage point, other faculty and administrators emphasized that a lack of explicit inclusion of international scholarship in Richmond's tenure and promotion policies does not inhibit faculty from internationalizing their teaching and research. Moreover, this group expressed that international scholarship should not be given priority over accomplishments in domestic or theoretical subject areas in Richmond's tenure and promotion policies. This group articulated that excellence in scholarship should remain the primary criterion in the tenure and promotion policies. In demonstration of this perspective, a senior administrative leader and two faculty offered the following comments:

[Faculty] say they should be rewarded for teaching about diversity. They should be rewarded for community service. They should be rewarded for international education. It really gets down to not a check off list for things you are rewarded for, but is your work uniformly excellent? (Senior administrative leader, personal communication, interview, May 3, 2007)

I just don't see any space at all between faculty involvement and teaching, research, and service that's internationally oriented and other kinds of activities.... I think there's a discussion in principle to be had there, as to whether one wants to distinguish internationally oriented work from what isn't, in that way. It's arguably an artificial, arbitrary line to draw. (Faculty member, personal communication, focus group, May 3, 2007)

I wouldn't want to distinguish out international teaching as opposed to some other kind of teaching. I really wouldn't want to create that kind of a rift. (Faculty member, focus group, personal communication, focus group, May 3, 2007)

Despite the varying views on this issue, there is evidence that some faculty perceive that without an explicit incorporation of international scholarship in Richmond's tenure and promotion policies, they are prompted to focus their attention on pursuing domestic and theoretical issues in their scholarship, which have traditionally been rewarded by these policies. Given this discord in perspectives about the importance of including international scholarship in tenure and promotion policies, a discussion of whether global perspectives is included in the definition of "excellence in scholarship" will be presented in a subsequent analysis section.

Summary

In sum, the organizational practices used at the University of Richmond to develop faculty engagement in internationalization include substantial investments in internationalization and the development of the Office of International Education (see Table 11). However, one organizational principle emerged that hindered the involvement of some faculty in internationalization: the lack of inclusion of international scholarship in Richmond's tenure and promotion policies.

Organizational Principles

Organizational principles refer to accepted codes of conduct that guide faculty teaching, research, and service. At the University of Richmond, the principles of interdisciplinarity and coordination encouraged faculty to participate in international initiatives.

Table 11. Richmond's Organizational Practices Used to Develop Faculty
Engagement in Internationalization

Strategies	Examples
Substantial investments in internationalization	Quest International Faculty Programming grants Curriculum internationalization grants Weinstein Grants for summer international projects
Development of Office of International Education	Academic standing of international education leader Strategic use of electronic resources Dramatic gestures and iconic moments

Interdisciplinarity

Interdisciplinarity was an organizational principle that opened the doors to international engagement for many faculty at the University of Richmond. Interdisciplinarity refers to research and teaching that occurs across two or more academic disciplines in the pursuit of a common goal, which may be perceived as too complex to be solved with the knowledge and methodologies of a single discipline. The 1986 internationalization plan served as a springboard to develop interdisciplinarity at Richmond, as the plan highlighted "the examination of international issues is done mostly on a discipline-specific basis, with little attention to cross-disciplinary dimensions or perspectives" (pp. 20-21). That admonition laid the groundwork for the interdisciplinary focus of three major programs at Richmond: the faculty seminar abroad, international studies program, and the Richmond Quest, which each will be discussed in turn.

The faculty seminar abroad has stimulated faculty to focus on the nexus of international and interdisciplinary education in numerous ways. In explaining the rationale for developing the faculty seminar abroad, Gabara described, "Internationalization in my mind is very strongly linked with interdisciplinarity. So, I felt we need to have [faculty] conversations across academic disciplines" (personal communication, interview, May 3, 2007). Accordingly, the seminar goals are to create opportunities for faculty to gain new international, interdisciplinary knowledge about a region or a country and involve faculty in interdisciplinary dialogues (University of Richmond Office of International Education, 2005b). Starting with the seminar application, faculty are encouraged to reflect on their involvement and interest in interdisciplinary and inter-school research and teaching (University of Richmond Office of International Education, 2007d). In the predeparture meetings, faculty are stimulated to discuss their disciplinary-based perspectives on the countries that will be visited. In demonstration of the interdisciplinary nature of the predeparture meetings, Gabara explained,

> The seminar is preceded by at least ten meetings [in which faculty] are presenting to each other about the country or region they are going to [visit] from their disciplinary perspectives. So, what they are learning from these sessions is…about the difference between what a historian will say about China and what an economist will say about China. (personal communication, interview, May 3, 2007)

While on the seminar abroad, faculty are prompted to engage in cross-disciplinary conversations, which have frequently resulted in the development of interdisciplinary teaching and research endeavors. Gabara explained,

> When you get a group of [faculty] from business to philosophy to art history various departments [who] are constantly talking to teach other [during the seminar], they stimulate each other's interests.… both about what they see and about the pedagogy of what happens on campus. Then they come back and the conversation continues. (personal communication, interview, May 3, 2007)

As this comment exemplifies, the organizational principle of interdisciplinarity is operationalized through Richmond's faculty seminar abroad, as it incubates faculty engagement in scholarly conversations beyond both national and disciplinary borders.

The international studies program is inherently interdisciplinary in nature, and, as such, has promoted the collaboration and networking of faculty from a wide range of disciplines. The interdisciplinary focus of the international studies programs grew out of the 1986 internationalization plan: This plan cited the importance of "designing an interdisciplinary curriculum in international studies" (p. 12), which would "require the contributions of faculty from several disciplines" (p. 18) and "contribute to an interdisciplinary exchange of approaches or methodologies" (p. 21). Through the development of the international studies program, a faculty member explained, "We started an interdisciplinary movement where we choose to proclaim that we did want to support people working at the margins of two different fields. International work is particularly amenable to that" (personal communication, focus group, May 3, 2007). As such, the international studies program has provided an avenue for faculty to engage in interdisciplinary scholarship.

In addition to the faculty seminar abroad and the international studies program, the "Richmond Quest" program has fueled the connection between faculty engagement in interdisciplinary and international scholarship. Every two years, Richmond's "Quest International" program has provided a new platform to reinvigorate faculty involvement in interdisciplinary and international scholarship. Through Quest International, faculty have been awarded grants to develop interdisciplinary, international courses and research that reflect the current Quest theme. In fact, the purpose of this well-endowed campus-wide initiative is "to explore and create unique synergies across our disciplines of arts and sciences, law, business, and leadership studies" (University of Richmond, 2007i, para. 4). Thus, through the Quest program, faculty have been presented with yet another mechanism through which to operationalize Richmond's interdisciplinarity, as well as internationalization plans.

Coordination

Coordination emerged as an organizational principle that supported faculty to engage in Richmond's internationalization. This principle underscores the significance of a centralized support system for planning, policy development, and information sharing. Coordination has been prominent in Richmond's culture and faculty engagement in internationalization, as evidenced through the 1986 internationalization plan, Office of International Education, international education committee, and 2006 strategic plan for international education.

Coordination is rooted in Richmond's 1986 internationalization plan, which promoted "the desirability of coordinating and expanding present activities at the University dealing with international studies" (p. 1). The 1986 internationalization plan noted, "The current administrative arrangements are haphazard. None of the personnel charged with overseeing international activities can give those duties even half their attention, and their efforts are poorly coordinated" (p. 11). In response to these concerns, the Office of International Education was established through the 1986 internationalization plan. This office has promoted the harmonization of faculty members' international initiatives across campus, by coordinating international teaching and research funding opportunities, the faculty seminar abroad, guidelines for taking students abroad, and the faculty international education survey (University of Richmond Office of International Education, 2007b).

The international education committee has stimulated coordination of international faculty activities by developing policies for international education initiatives that take place on campus and overseas. The committee, which was established by the 1986 plan, has the following charge issued by the provost, to whom the committee reports:

> The International Education Committee develops policies for international education, including educational opportunities on campus and study abroad programs. It refers academic issues to the faculty and recommends policies to the administration for approval, as appropriate. It is also responsible for overseeing the implementation of such policies. (University of Richmond Office of the Provost, 2007)

Gabara highlighted, "The charge of the committee is really to oversee the implementation of internationalization policies across the five schools of the university" (personal communication, interview, May 3, 2007). A faculty member described that this committee has functioned as a "board of directors," as it has focused on evaluating and approving new international programs and courses, and allocating funding for international initiatives across campus (Faculty member, personal communication, focus group, May 3, 2007). Another faculty member clarified, "To me, [the committee] has a functional, structural role in the [internationalization of the university] that is in part advisory to Uliana and in part just has certain functions that need to be carried out.... such as reading applications for internationalization grants" (personal communication, focus group, May 3, 2007). Moreover, an exchange between a university administrator and faculty member highlighted the symbolic function served by the committee: An administrator explained the international education committee reflects "an area of recognition, an area of focus that is important to the university." A faculty member responded, "And, we know it is, because there is a committee for it. So, it's got to be real" (personal communications, focus group, May 3, 2007).

Finally, the 2006 strategic plan for international education further operationalized the principle of coordination at Richmond, as the plan recommended the creation of an "International Living and Learning Center" on campus "to bring together the expanding array of international programs and activities for increased synergy and visibility" (p. 2). By seeking to provide a centralized space for international programs that are currently "isolated around the university" (p. 2), the 2006 plan furthers the coordination of faculty involvement in international activities. Overall, as exemplified by this internationalization plan and the international education committee coordination served as an organizational principle that has supported faculty engagement in Richmond's internationalization.

Summary

In sum, two organizational principles emerged as accepted codes of conduct that guided faculty involvement in internationalization. These organizational principles were interdisciplinarity and coordination. Table 12 provides a synthesis and examples of these principles.

Table 12. Richmond's Organizational Principles Used to Develop Faculty Engagement in Internationalization

Organizational principles	Examples
Interdisciplinarity	Faculty seminar abroad International studies program Richmond Quest program
Coordination	Office of International Education International education committee

Internationalization Plans

In this section, the University of Richmond's internationalization plan types, internationalization plan roles, and the alignment of faculty engagement strategies articulated in Richmond's multiple internationalization plans will be presented.

Internationalization Plan Types

Two of the internationalization plan types, according to the researcher's internationalization plan typology (see Appendix), were found at the University of Richmond. First, Richmond has incorporated internationalization into its current university strategic plan (2000). Second, Richmond has developed two documents that have served as distinct internationalization plans (1986, 2006). All three of these internationalization plans detail various strategies to develop faculty engagement in international scholarship.

Internationalization Plan Roles

Richmond's internationalization plans served the following roles in increasing faculty engagement in internationalization: (a) develop coordination, (b) express intentionality, and (c) allocate resources. In illustration of the coordination role, the 1986 internationalization plan developed the coordinating infrastructure to support faculty involvement in international activities through the establishment of the Office of International Education and the international education committee. Furthermore, the 2006 internationalization plan advocated for the creation of an International Living and Learning Center to create a centralized physical structure for faculty engaging in international teaching and research.

In demonstration of the plan's expression of intentionality, the 1986 internationalization plan emphasized the "encouragement of faculty and course development in international studies" (p. 13). In 2006, the university's second internationalization plan articulated Richmond's commitment to advance this goal and "further internationalize the curricula and programs in each of the University's schools" (p. 2).

In addition, both internationalization plans emphasized the allocation of resources to support faculty engagement in internationalization. The 1986 internationalization plan indicated a commitment for the international education committee to work with the offices of development and sponsored programs to allocate funds to support faculty engagement in international scholarship. Moreover, the 2006 internationalization plan identified the office of international education's allocation of "funding in support of the development of new courses with significant international content" (p. 2).

Overall, internationalization plans have developed infrastructural support for faculty to coordinate their internationalization resources and agendas, expressed intentionally the institutional goal for faculty to internationalize their scholarship, and allocated resources for faculty to take steps to implement this goal.

Internationalization Plan Alignment

The alignment of faculty engagement strategies in Richmond's internationalization plans is indicated in Table 13. Each of Richmond's internationalization plans, three in total, details various strategies to develop faculty engagement in international scholarship. In particular, three of Richmond's faculty engagement strategies were articulated in two internationalization plans. These strategies included the intentional hiring of faculty with international expertise, development of international faculty seminars, and funding resources for international initiatives. As such, the alignment of these strategies in different internationalization plans supported faculty involvement in the operationalization of Richmond's internationalization plans, as support and reinforcement was given at multiple institutional levels.

Summary

In sum, two of the three types of internationalization represented in the researcher's internationalization plan typology were found at the University of Richmond. These plans have promoted faculty involvement in international activities by developing coordination, expressing intentionality, and allocating resources. Moreover, out of the 11 faculty engagement strategies, three were included in two different types of plans. As such, faculty were encouraged at multiple institutional levels to engage in the operationalization of Richmond's internationalization goals.

Table 13. Alignment of Strategies Articulated in Richmond's
        Internationalization Plans

Strategy	Internationalization plans	
	Number of	Types of
Hiring	3	USP, IP(1), IP(2)
Faculty seminars	2	USP, IP(2)
Funding resources	2	IP(1), IP(2)
Internationally focused committees	1	IP(1)
Alignment with university diversity initiative	1	IP(2)
Departmental collaborations	1	IP(1)
Office of International Education	1	IP(1)
Recommended development of International Living and Learning Center	1	IP(2)
International studies program	1	IP(1)
Recommended inclusion of internationalization in tenure and promotion policies	1	IP(2)

Note. USP= university strategic plan (2001); IP(1)= internationalization plan (1986); IP(2)= internationalization plan (2006).

Table 14. Synthesis of Richmond's Strategies Used to Develop Faculty
        Engagement in Internationalization

Academic activities	Organizational practices	Organizational principles
Faculty seminars	Substantial investments in internationalization	Interdisciplinarity
International teaching opportunities	Development of Office of International Education	Coordination

University of Richmond Case Study Summary

In summary, this section presented the story of the University of Richmond's development of faculty engagement in internationalization. The findings emerged from the interviews, focus groups, and documentation conducted for this study. Table 14 presents a synthesis of the academic activities, organizational practices, and organizational principles that supported faculty engagement in Richmond's internationalization.

Two types of internationalization plans, according to the researcher's internationalization plan typology, were found at Richmond: university strategic plans and distinct documents. The three overarching roles these plans served in developing faculty engagement in Richmond's internationalization were to (a) develop coordination (b) express intentionality, and (c) allocate resources. Finally, out of 11 faculty engagement strategies, three were articulated in more than one internationalization plan, thus multiplying the support for faculty involvement in international activities at various institutional levels.

Cross-Case Findings and Analysis

This section presents a comparison and analysis of findings across Duke University and the University of Richmond. Like the individual case study sections, this section is organized by the following subtopics: (a) context, (b) academic activities, (c) organizational practices, (d) organizational principles, and (e) types and alignment of internationalization plans that have affected faculty engagement in internationalization.

Context

Five contextual variables were central to the development of faculty engagement in internationalization at Duke and Richmond: (a) endowment size and special allocations, (b) institutional size, (c) senior institutional leaders' support, (d) types of institutional stakeholders who spearheaded internationalization plans, (e) multiple institutional levels at which internationalization plans were developed, and (f) student influence. These variables will be discussed in turn, after which the unexpected lack of influence of campus-wide committees will be analyzed.

Endowment Size and Special Allocations

The large endowments of Duke and Richmond—$4.6 billion and $1.6 billion, respectively (Duke University Office of News and Communications, 2007; National Association of College and University Business Officers,

2007; University of Richmond Advancement Office, 2007)—supported the development of faculty engagement in internationalization. As a little funding goes a long way to promote internationalization, these cases illuminate specific types of funding that generated long-term support for faculty engagement in internationalization at Duke and Richmond. In particular, Duke's endowed funds for distinguished international visitors, such as the Karl von der Heyden International Fellows Program Endowment, Semans Professorship for Distinguished International Visiting Scholars Endowment, and the Bernstein Memorial International and Comparative Law Endowment, supported faculty in developing international scholarly collaborations. Likewise, Richmond's endowed funds for international faculty activities, such as the Weinstein Grants for Summer International Projects, supported Richmond faculty to conduct cross-cultural teaching, research, and service projects in the US and overseas. As such, not only did the size of Duke and Richmond's endowments provide support for faculty to participate in their institutions' internationalization, but specially endowed funds targeted for international scholarship created visibility and incentives for faculty to engage in their institution's internationalization.

These findings provide an important gloss on the internationalization scholars' acknowledgment that funding matters (e.g., Backman, 1984; Bond, 2003; Green & Olson, 2003). At Duke and Richmond, not only did funding matter, but targeted funding mattered, especially where that funding was differentially invested in internationalization. In short, it was not only the amount of funds, but how they were invested that was critical in the development of faculty engagement in internationalization at Duke and Richmond. Both institution's strategic investments in their internationalization plans created opportunities for faculty to connect their unique scholarly agendas with the internationalization plan goals. Because there were a variety of kinds of investments, e.g., international centers, seminars, curriculum integration grants, distinguished scholar endowments, there were a multitude of types of resources for faculty to choose from to augment the international focus of their scholarship. The upshot of this finding is that higher education institutions and scholars examining those institutions need to take account of the impact that targeted investment strategies may have on longer-term goals of internationalization.

Institutional Size

The contextual comparison of Duke and Richmond synthesized in Table 15 demonstrates Duke's larger institutional size in terms of acreage, schools, faculty and student populations, and endowment created a substratum for decentralized faculty engagement strategies to thrive. Moreover, Richmond's smaller institutional size in terms of the aforementioned components provided a foundation from which centralized strategies surfaced as highly influential in developing faculty involvement in internationalization.

Table 15. Cross-Case Analysis Institutional Size Information

Institutional characteristics	Duke University	University of Richmond
Geographic Size	9,000 acres	350 acres
Schools	9	5
Endowment	$4.5 billion	$1.6 billion
Undergraduate Students	6,197	2,857
Graduate and Professional Students	6,627	697
Tenured or Tenure-track Faculty	1,667	242
Number of Regular-rank Faculty	997	140

Note. Data were derived from "Quick Facts about Duke University," by Duke University Office of News and Communication, 2007; "Fast Facts," by University of Richmond, 2007; and "2006 NACUBO Endowment Study," by National Association of College and University Business Officers, 2007.

As Duke faculty are dispersed throughout 9,000 acres and nine schools, even though the university has a central international office, centralized strategies to develop faculty engagement in internationalization would not be most effective. Rather, because of Duke's size, a series of decentralized strategies, including Duke's (a) Title VI and other international and area studies centers and (b) integration of internationalization into the nine schools' strategic plans, enabled faculty from a wide range of disciplines to connect their disparate scholarly agendas with Duke's internationalization goals. For example, the Center for International and Comparative Law located in Duke Law School and the Center for International Business Education and Research located in Duke's Fuqua Business School provide faculty with international scholarly resources that are customized to their disciplinary interests. In addition, area studies centers, such as the Asian/Pacific Studies Institute and the Center for Latin American and Caribbean Studies, provide faculty with resources customized to their regional interests. Notably, through the integration of internationalization into each of the schools' strategic plans, connections between disciplinary priorities and internationalization were made explicit and resources for faculty to pursue those connections were allocated. Thus, although Duke's international initiatives are decentralized, they are aligned with individual school priorities and overarching internationalization goals for the institution through the development and alignment of Duke's three types of internationalization plans.

Richmond's relatively smaller institutional size, i.e., faculty are dispersed throughout only 350 acres and five schools, enabled the university's central international office—the Office of International Education—to develop centralized strategies to support widespread faculty engagement in internationalization. For example, this central office has streamlined the availability and organization of resources for faculty to engage in international teaching research, and service through its (a) faculty seminar abroad, (b) Web resources, (c) curriculum international grants, and (d) regular electronic communications targeted to increase faculty members' integration of international and return study abroad students into their classroom discussions.

In short, institutional size affected the strategies used to develop faculty involvement in internationalization. Because Duke's faculty are spread out on more than 25 times more acres and almost double the amount of schools, strategies that provided support for Duke's subunits to customize internationalization goals to their disciplinary and regional priorities enabled faculty on this decentralized campus to connect with the institution's overarching goals for internationalization. Moreover, due to its smaller campus, Richmond's central international office was enabled to create awareness of faculty at large about international opportunities and target individual faculty with resources to advance the internationalization of their particular areas of scholarship. Thus, at Duke and Richmond the development of faculty engagement took account of organic institutional characteristics, not only limited to size, but also the number of subunits and schools as well as the physical space.

Senior Leaders' Support

At Duke and Richmond, senior institutional leaders provided support for faculty to engage in international initiatives. At both institutions, provosts led the development of committees that created the institutions' internationalization plans. Moreover, at Duke University, the presidents' and board of trustees' support was influential. In particular, recent presidents encouraged faculty to explore international dimensions in their scholarly agendas by shining their presidential spotlights on internationalization in their rhetoric and commitment of resources. Furthermore, Duke's board of trustees shined its spotlight on internationalization by approving it as a priority in the university's recent strategic plans (2000, 2006) and committing resources to support faculty engagement in the operationalization of the university's internationalization plans. As such, this study affirms the findings of the American Council on Education study, "Promising Practices: Spotlighting Excellence in Comprehensive Internationalization" (Engberg & Green, 2002), which found that comprehensive internationalization is advanced at institutions whose presidents and chief academic officers are "ardent supporters and public champions of internationalization" (p. 11).

Essentially, senior leaders' support was highly influential in developing faculty engagement. With the support of provosts, presidents, and boards of trustees came consistent signals that (a) internationalization was central to the institutions' mission; (b) faculty involvement was, therefore, critical to its success; and (c) financial and programmatic resources were available to enable faculty to participate in the implementation of the institutions' internationalization plans.

Types of Stakeholders Who Spearheaded Internationalization Plans

Interestingly, Duke and Richmond's internationalization plans were spearheaded by different types of institutional stakeholders. At Duke, the larger, more decentralized institution, development of the institution's first internationalization plan was precipitated through a faculty initiative: In response to the fall of the Berlin Wall, in 1989, a multidisciplinary group of faculty approached a senior administrative leader—the provost—about the importance of focusing on the internationalization of the university. This initial faculty involvement set the foundation for institutional support for faculty-driven international initiatives. However, at Richmond, the smaller, more centralized institution, the internationalization plan development was spearheaded through the initiative of a senior administrative leader: After attending an academic deans' conference that addressed the concept of "international competence," Richmond's arts and sciences dean gathered a multidisciplinary group of faculty to determine the meaning and plans for development of "international competence" at the University of Richmond.

Despite these differences in the type of institutional stakeholder—senior administrative leader or faculty—who initiated the process, immediately thereafter, a multidisciplinary faculty committee was charged by a senior administrative leader to develop an internationalization plan for the university in both cases. Because this charge was issued by a senior administrative leader, institutional support, such as the development of infrastructure and allocation of resources, was infused into not only the development, but implementation of the internationalization plans at both institutions. As such, this support from senior administrative leaders was crucial to the development of widespread faculty engagement in internationalization at Duke and Richmond.

Multiple Institutional Levels at which Internationalization Plans Were Developed

The development of internationalization plans at multiple institutional levels advanced faculty engagement in internationalization at both institutions. At Duke and Richmond, not only did the institutions develop a series of two successive internationalization plans, but they also integrated internationalization into the university strategic plans. In so doing, both institutions fortified their commitments to internationalization by integrating the value of international scholarship into the policy documents that guide the work of academic deans and senior administrative leaders.

Yet, Duke University took the development of the university's internationalization plans one step further. Because internationalization was identified as one of six institutional priorities in the university strategic plan (2006), the president and provost charged all of Duke's nine school deans to integrate internationalization into their schools' strategic plans. As such, through the development of unit plans for internationalization, the president and provost facilitated the support of the schools' deans in internationalization and encouraged their allocation of resources at the school level. As faculty tend to focus their teaching and research agendas based on the current priorities of their departments and disciplines, the integration of internationalization into schools' strategic plans provided a critical link through which institutional priorities for internationalization were adapted to disciplinary concerns. Thus, through the symbolic, programmatic, and financial support provided by these unit plans for internationalization, disciplinary connections to internationalization were made explicit, which promoted widespread faculty engagement in internationalization.

Ultimately, internationalization plans mattered because they expressed intentional commitments to integrate international perspectives into the teaching, research, and service functions of the institution. As such, they led to the development and allocation of resources for faculty of all disciplines to internationalize their scholarship. Importantly, the plans reflected the organic realities of each institution. Through iterative processes that engaged an interdisciplinary group of faculty to discuss what internationalization means at the institution, institutional strengths and weaknesses relating to that customized definition, and particular goals to advance the institutions' internationalization, internationalization plans were developed to address Duke and

Richmond's unique institutional needs, based on institutional type, size, history, culture, mission, and resources.

Student Influence

Students served an important role at Duke and Richmond in motivating faculty to integrate international dimensions into their work. At both institutions, faculty highlighted that their students' inquiries stimulated them to globalize their curricula, add international cases to their course discussions and syllabi, and explore international dimensions in their research. Moreover, Duke faculty emphasized that advising students' about their international service projects and Richmond faculty indicated that advising students about their study abroad opportunities provided countless occasions to explore the value of international perspectives in their disciplines with students. As such, at both institutions, internationally oriented students brought international issues into discussions with faculty both inside and outside of the classroom, which prompted faculty to engage in their institutions' internationalization.

In essence, student demand was critical in developing faculty engagement in Duke and Richmond's internationalization. Because it was commonplace for Duke and Richmond students to introduce international perspectives and topics into discussions with faculty both inside and outside the classroom, students prompted their faculty to consider their disciplines from multiple cultural vantage points. Although institutional leaders may not have been aware about the power of students in terms of developing faculty engagement in internationalization, students' awareness of and interests in cross-cultural perspectives created gateways to faculty engagement in internationalization.

Lack of Influence of Campus-wide Internationalization Committees

Although internationalization experts suggested that campus-wide internationalization committees serve important organizational roles to facilitate widespread faculty involvement in internationalization (e.g., Back et al., 1996; Backman, 1984; Harari, 1981; Thullen et al., 2002), this did not prove to be the case at Duke or Richmond. Rather, whereas Duke and Richmond's campus-wide internationalization committees served critical roles in the development of internationalization plans to address broad university needs, additional organizational mechanisms, including academic activities, organizational practices, and organizational principles, which will be discussed in subsequent sections, replaced campus-wide committees as critical factors that developed widespread faculty involvement in the implementation of internationalization plans.

To understand the less influential role than expected of internationalization committees on the implementation of internationalization plans, it is useful to analyze the charge of these committees. At Duke, the "Provost's Executive Committee for International Affairs" was charged with the task of "providing a plan of internationalization that could be integrated with Duke University's overall strategic plan" (Duke University Provost's Executive Committee for International Affairs, 1995, p. iii). The current incarnation of this Duke committee, the International Affairs Committee, is charged with providing coordination and exchange of information across schools and international units, such as the international visa office, intercultural programming office, and international and area studies centers. It is important to note that the power of these Duke committees has been limited to advisory functions, so that the flow of information is largely among committee members and from the committee to the senior administration, e.g., the provost. Moreover, it is important to note that the charge of these committees was not to oversee the implementation of Duke's internationalization plans. Therefore, as a senior administrative leader at Duke expressed, "There is a gap between the committee and the enterprise of individual faculty" (personal communication, interview, May 8, 2007).

Richmond's "Ad Hoc Committee on International Studies" was charged in 1983 by the arts and sciences dean to define international competence and offer recommendations about how Richmond can help undergraduate students acquire it (Tremaine, 1994). This ad hoc committee recommended the development of Richmond's current "International Education Committee," which reports to the provost and is charged with developing policies for international education, referring academic issues to the faculty, policies to the administration for approval, and overseeing the implementation of such policies (University of Richmond Office of the Provost, 2007). Although this is the committee's official charge, study participants described the main focus of the committee is to advise the international education dean on international education policies and review and allocate funding for faculty and students' international initiative proposals. Yet, Richmond's international education committee did develop an "Internationalization Plan Taskforce" in 2006 to develop updated goals and recommendations for internationalization (University of Richmond International Education Committee, 2006c). However, neither the International Education Committee nor the Internationalization Plan Taskforce was charged with the implementation of Richmond's internationalization plan.

Therefore, Duke and Richmond's internationalization committees mattered only to a limited extent in developing widespread faculty engagement in the implementation of internationalization plans. Duke and Richmond's internationalization committees were critical in providing structural support for an interdisciplinary group of faculty to develop the institutions' internationalization plans. However, after the plans were created, implementation emerged not through the direct actions of the committees but rather through the array of academic activities, organizational practices, and organizational principles throughout the institutions that provided support for faculty to connect their scholarly agendas with the internationalization goals. Due to the limitations in their charges, committees mattered in the development but not the operationalization of Duke and Richmond's internationalization plans. Recommendations for how to address these limitations are offered in Chapter V.

Context Summary

Essentially, targeted funds, institutional size, student demand, and internationalization plans mattered in the development of faculty engagement in internationalization at Duke and Richmond. Despite Duke and Richmond's differences in institutional type and size, specially allocated endowment funds created a fulcrum through which faculty engaged in international initiatives. Moreover, because an interdisciplinary group of faculty were involved with the drafting of Duke and Richmond's internationalization plans, their corresponding strategies for faculty engagement took into consideration diverse faculty interests and priorities. Yet, implementation of the internationalization plans emerged from the supportive infrastructure developed at both institutions, in the form of academic activities, organizational practices, and organizational principles. Further, the more institutional levels at which internationalization plans were developed at Duke and Richmond, i.e., integrated into university strategic plans, developed as distinct university-wide documents, and integrated into subunit strategic plans, the more support for faculty to connect their individual scholarly agendas was provided. Finally, student interest motivated faculty involvement in international scholarship.

Academic Activities

Academic activities encouraged faculty engagement in international scholarship, by providing opportunities for faculty to integrate international dimensions into their teaching and research. At both universities, academic activities, including (a) faculty seminars and (b) international teaching opportunities, facilitated faculty participation in the implementation of their institutions' internationalization plans.

Faculty Seminars

Duke and Richmond's faculty seminars shared similar and distinct components that supported faculty to pursue international scholarship. Because both institutions' faculty seminars were (a) sponsored by well-regarded university centers, (b) included an interdisciplinary focus, and (c) incorporated timing and faculty commitment considerations, they promoted the engagement of faculty in internationalization at Duke and Richmond. Yet, as Richmond required pre-seminar group study and teaching, this served as an additional embedded strategy, which developed faculty knowledge and awareness of cross-cultural perspectives within their disciplines and augmented their preparation for and participation in the faculty seminar abroad.

Sponsored by well-regarded university centers. Due to the sponsorship of faculty seminars by well-regarded university centers, the seminars served as useful mechanisms to encourage latent faculty supporters of internationalization to consider integrating international perspectives into their scholarship. Even faculty with no prior interest in internationalization tended to have respect for and interest in the work of these well-regarded university centers: At Duke, the Social Science Research Institute and John Hope Franklin Humanities Institute, which were widely viewed as prestigious institutes among faculty from diversity of disciplines, sponsored various faculty seminars on diverse international themes. At Richmond, the Office of International Education, which had strong connections with departments and faculty throughout the institution, sponsored the highly valued faculty seminar abroad. At each institution, these seminars prompted faculty from disciplines that were traditionally domestically focused to explore cross-cultural perspectives within their scholarship.

Interdisciplinary focus. The interdisciplinary emphasis of Duke and Richmond's faculty seminars provided support for latent faculty supporters to engage in their institution's internationalization. As internationalization scholars have noted, divisions between disciplines can preclude the interdisciplinary collaboration that is increasingly important to operationalize internationalization plans (e.g., Bond, 2003; Ellingboe, 1998). Yet, interdisciplinarity was an underlying organizational principle that was valued by faculty throughout both institutions. Therefore, the interdisciplinary focus of Duke and Richmond's faculty seminars provided avenues through which faculty who had not considered integrating international perspectives, but had considered integrating interdisciplinary perspectives, were prompted to explore both the cross-disciplinary and transnational dimensions of their teaching and research agendas.

Timing and commitment considerations. Both Duke and Richmond's faculty seminars included timing and commitment considerations that made it feasible and attractive for faculty to participate. At both institutions, faculty expressed that the primary obstacle to their participation in international activities was not money, but time. Accordingly, Duke addressed the high demands on faculty time by incorporating teaching release time as a component of faculty members' participation in the aforementioned institutes' semester- or year-long, residential seminars. Richmond addressed the pressure on faculty time in a different way. As opposed to conducting the seminars during the regular academic year, Richmond's faculty seminar abroad was conducted over a period of three weeks during the summer. As such, Richmond's seminar did not impose on faculty teaching commitments during the academic year and still left plenty of time for faculty to focus on their research agendas during the summer. Overall, though their timing and commitment considerations, Duke and Richmond addressed a major inhibitor of faculty participation in internationalization—lack of time—by carving out time for faculty to internationalize their scholarship.

Required pre-seminar group study and teaching. Because Richmond's faculty seminar abroad uniquely required participants to study cultural and disciplinary materials relating, as well as teach key components to their participant colleagues in pre-seminar workshops, this addressed the concern that faculty need specific knowledge in order to engage in internationalization. As such, the inclusion of pre-seminar requirements presented a strategy through which Richmond addressed this faculty engagement challenge.

International Teaching Opportunities

Like the faculty seminars, Duke and Richmond developed similar and distinct international teaching opportunities that supported their faculty to engage in internationalization. Although both institutions developed international degree programs, Duke's campus overseas and Richmond's support for faculty to integrate study abroad into their work provided unique opportunities through which faculty engaged in internationalization.

International degree programs. International degree programs at both institutions provided infrastructural support for faculty to engage in international teaching. Both institutions' programs (i.e., the Duke University/ Frankfurt University Executive MBA, Duke's Global Executive MBA, Duke's JD/LLM in Comparative and International Law, and Richmond's

International Studies BA) structured opportunities for faculty to explore international issues in their classrooms on campus. Additionally, Duke's programs integrated opportunities for their faculty to teach overseas through its professional international degree programs in business and law. Through these programs, faculty developed and taught courses such as "Local Laws, Global Problems: Conflict of Laws and the Challenge of Globalization," "International and Comparative Taxation," and "Rights of Racial Groups and Indigenous Peoples" (Duke University School of Law, 2007a, 2007c). Thus, as faculty prioritize their teaching agendas based upon institutional and disciplinary support, international degree programs created forums through which faculty were encouraged to explore international dimensions of their disciplines with students in classrooms on the home campus and overseas.

Development of an overseas campus. Moreover, Duke's development of an overseas medical campus—the Duke University/National University of Singapore Graduate Medical School—provided additional opportunities for faculty to participate in not only international teaching, but research and curriculum development. As a result, this international collaboration has enabled Duke faculty to engage in research and teaching on prominent healthcare issues in Singapore and in Asia, as well as pursue transnational, biomedical research that would not otherwise be easily accessible to Duke faculty (Williams, 2007). Although Richmond did not develop campuses abroad, Richmond faculty were not without opportunities to teach overseas. In fact, at Richmond, faculty were presented with institutional resources to (a) lead and teach on summer study abroad programs and (b) integrate study abroad components into their courses.

Summer study abroad programs. Long-standing opportunities for faculty to lead and teach on Richmond's study abroad programs have institutionalized support for faculty to engage in international teaching. Just as short-term study abroad programs have been lauded for providing opportunities for students who would not otherwise venture overseas to gain international exposure (e.g., Lewis & Niesenbaum, 2005; Sindt & Pachmayer, 2005; Taylor, 1997), summer study abroad programs provide short-term opportunities for faculty who would not be likely to travel abroad due to personal and professional commitments to increase their international awareness and experiences.

Support to integrate study abroad into on-campus courses. Richmond's support for faculty to integrate study abroad into on-campus courses has served as a strategy, albeit a seemingly oxymoronic one, which has encouraged faculty from a wide range of disciplines to internationalize their syllabi. In addition to leading and teaching summer study abroad programs, Richmond faculty have received support to add a one- or two-week overseas study component to an otherwise on-campus course. Like the summer study abroad programs, this curricular integration support enables faculty to participate in teaching overseas without making a long-term commitment. However, unlike the summer study abroad programs, integrating study abroad into on campus classes prompts faculty to address cross-cultural comparisons in their syllabi and teaching both on campus and overseas.

As faculty are pivotal in the internationalization of the curriculum, by providing support for faculty to integrate study abroad into on-campus courses, Richmond has developed a unique strategy designed to address endogenous constraints on faculty time and commitments and thereby promote faculty engagement in the internationalization of their curricula.

Academic Activities Summary

Academic activities facilitated faculty engagement in internationalization through their provision of a variety of disciplinary and interdisciplinary opportunities. In particular, interdisciplinary seminars provided well-timed opportunities for faculty to explore international themes within and across disciplines and develop collaborations to integrate international perspectives into their scholarship. Moreover, international degree programs provided opportunities for faculty to incorporate international perspectives into their teaching both on and off campus. Finally, study abroad programs and curricular integration support enabled faculty to teach abroad for short periods of time and integrate study abroad components into on-campus courses, thereby taking into account the significant demands on faculty time.

In short, Duke and Richmond's academic activities provided critical opportunities for faculty to engage directly in the integration of international perspectives into their teaching and research. While faculty seminars supported faculty to develop knowledge, skills, and collaborations to internationalize their research, opportunities to teach overseas and teach in international degree programs on campus supported faculty to internationalize their curricula. As a result, academic activities both on campus and overseas facilitated the engagement of Duke and Richmond faculty in their institutions' internationalization.

Organizational Practices

Organizational practices encouraged faculty engagement in Duke and Richmond's internationalization, by providing critical infrastructure, incentives, and communication mechanisms to support faculty in developing international dimensions in their teaching and research. As indicated by Table 16, organizational practices such as (a) differential investments in internationalization and (b) strategic use of electronic communication channels. However, one organizational practice inhibited faculty engagement in internationalization: the lack of inclusion of internationally-focused scholarship in tenure and promotion policies.

Table 16. Cross-Case Comparison of Organizational Practices that Developed Faculty Engagement in Internationalization

Organizational practice	Duke University	University of Richmond
Substantial financial investments in internationalization	X	X
Strategic use of electronic resources	X	X
Reaccreditation self-study	X	
Development of decentralized international centers	X	
Development of centralized international office		X

Differential Investments in Internationalization Plans

The differential investments in internationalization plans at multiple institutional levels and through a variety of funding sources undergirded Duke and Richmond's development of faculty engagement in internationalization. Differential investment in internationalization plans is the process of allocating and diversifying resources in various increments, types, and locations throughout an institution in order to develop the engagement of key stakeholders, so that the internationalization plans become operationalized. As a lack of financial resources prevents the development of incentives for faculty to engage in international Activities, Duke and Richmond have addressed this institutional challenge through distributing responsibility for financial support of faculty engagement through multiple institutional levels and through soliciting support from a variety of types of sources (e.g., federal, private, and institutional).

At Duke and Richmond, funding to support faculty engagement in internationalization has not been the responsibility of only the central international office (see Table 17). Rather the responsibility for supporting faculty engagement in internationalization has been disseminated among various institutional units (e.g., president's office, provost's office, central international office, and individual schools and centers). Funding has been solicited from a variety of sources, including US Department of Education programs (e.g., Duke's Title VI faculty international research and conference travel grants) and alumni endowed contributions (e.g., Duke's "Bernstein Memorial International and Comparative Law Endowment" and Richmond's "Weinstein Summer International Project Grants"). Moreover, the alignment of internationalization with other institution-wide initiatives (e.g., Richmond's "Quest International" and Duke's "Global Health" initiatives) has also promoted the dispersement of international resources to faculty. For example, Duke's "Global Health" initiative has provided $5,000 travel awards for faculty pursuing global health research. Thus, through the alignment of internationalization with other institution-wide initiatives, various sources of funding, and dispersement of resources at multiple institutional levels, differential investment has enabled Duke and Richmond faculty to engage in the implementation of their institutions' internationalization plans.

Strategic Use of Electronic Communication Channels

Duke and Richmond's central international offices' strategic use of electronic communication channels has facilitated faculty engagement in the institutions' internationalization plans. These communication channels took various forms, including an international faculty database system and international blogs at Duke, and electronic examples of internationalized syllabi and a faculty internationalization survey at Richmond. Given faculty members' frequent use of electronic media, Duke and Richmond's electronic communications channels provided vehicles for (a) central offices to convey international information and resources to faculty and (b) central offices to collect information about faculty members' areas of international expertise and interests. Additionally, Duke has provided mechanisms for faculty to share international resources with each other within and across disciplines, which has increased faculty engagement in internationalization.

Table 17. Differential Investments in Faculty Engagement
in Internationalization

Institutional level	Example	Amount
President	Richmond's "Quest International" faculty programming and course development grants	$10,000 for international curricular and co-curricular endeavors $3,500 for new course developments $1,500 for existing course revisions
Provost	Full funding for Richmond's Faculty Seminar Abroad	$50,000 (every two years for 10-12 faculty)
School	Richmond's School of Arts & Sciences Overseas Conference Travel Grants	$1,200
Central International Office	Richmond's Weinstein Grants for Summer International Projects	$15,000 for existing course revisions
Office of Study Abroad	Duke's Office of Study Abroad Curriculum Integration Initiative	$4,000 for new course developments $5000 for exchange university site visits and international conference attendance
International Centers	Duke's Title VI Faculty Research and Conference International Travel Grants	$500 for presentation on Latin American topics at US conferences $750 for presentation on Latin American topics at overseas conferences $5,000 for development of conference on Asian theme $3,000 for development of course on Asian theme $2,500 for research on Asian theme

First, through the strategic use of electronic communication channels, central offices, such as Duke's Office of the Vice Provost for International Affairs (OVPIA) and Richmond's Office of International Education (OIE), created electronic gateways that centralized international resources for faculty. As such, at both institutions, faculty were given a clear mechanism through which to become informed about international opportunities. For example, on the faculty resources section of Richmond's OIE Web page, faculty have had access to (a) funding resources for international teaching, research, and service, (b) internationalized syllabi examples, (b) foreign faculty hiring information, and (c) guidelines for taking students overseas.

Second, the strategic electronic communication channels have enabled central offices to gain awareness of faculty members' areas of international expertise and interests. Thus, Duke's OVPIA and Richmond's OIE Web sites have served not only as gateways for these central international offices to inform faculty about international resources but also as mediums through which these central offices collect information about faculty. For example, through the "international education faculty survey" on Richmond's OIE Web site, OIE has regularly collected information about faculty members' international expertise and interests. As such, OIE has been enabled to target international opportunities to specific faculty based upon their regional and topical regional research interests.

Third, Duke's strategic use of electronic communication channels has enabled faculty to share international resources within and across disciplines. In so doing, Duke has addressed a prevalent challenge that a lack of intra- and interdisciplinary communication channels can inhibit the collaboration that is important for faculty engagement in internationalization. For example, Duke's OVPIA and Global Health Institute Web pages have provided faculty with forums through which to communicate their international scholarly interests and experiences with their colleagues. Through the international faculty database system housed on Duke's OVPIA Web page, faculty are provided with a mechanism through which to search for colleagues within and across disciplines who are engaged in research on specific topics, countries, or regions. As an important component of international scholarship is collaboration across nations and disciplines, this database has enabled faculty to identify and communicate with colleagues about international matters of mutual interest. In addition, both Duke's Global Health Institute and OVPIA Web pages have provided faculty with forums through which to develop international blogs to share their global health and other international teaching, research, and service experiences.

Through Duke and Richmond's strategic use of communication channels, feedback loops were created so that information, resources, and opportunities were conveyed at multiple institutional levels, i.e. from central international offices to faculty, from faculty to central international offices, and among faculty (see Figure 2). Just as Birnbaum (1988) demonstrated the importance of feedback loops in academic administration in general (as discussed in Chapter II), this study illuminates their importance in two institutions' development of faculty engagement in internationalization in particular. Overall, Duke and Richmond's strategic use of the Internet and other forms of electronic communication greased the wheels of the feedback loops, which increased faculty awareness of and participation in international initiatives that advanced their own scholarly agendas and their institutions' internationalization plans.

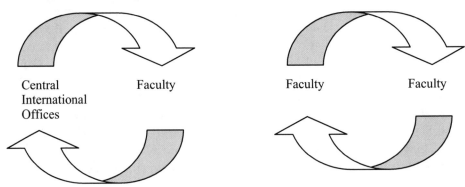

Central　　　　　Faculty　　　　　　Faculty　　　　　Faculty
International
Offices

Figure 2. Critical feedback loops for faculty engagement in internationalization

Lack of Inclusion of Internationally-Focused Scholarship in Tenure and Promotion Policies

One organizational practice emerged not as a facilitator but as an inhibitor of faculty engagement in internationalization: the lack of inclusion of internationally-focused scholarship in tenure and promotion policies. Although internationalization scholars concur that the lack of an explicit inclusion of international scholarship in tenure and promotion policies presents disincentives for faculty to focus on the internationalization of their teaching, research, and service (e.g., Backman, 1981; Carter, 1992; Ellingboe, 1998; E. L. Miller, 1992; Siaya & Hayward, 2003; Viers, 1998), the results of this study confirmed this contention for some Duke and Richmond faculty and revealed an alternate perspective held by other faculty and senior administrative leaders at the institutions.

Whereas the lack of inclusion of international scholarship in Duke and Richmond's tenure and promotion policies created disincentives for some junior, tenure-track faculty to concentrate on integrating international perspectives into their scholarship, tenured faculty indicated their aversion to treating international scholarship as different from any other scholarship. This latter group of faculty expressed that "excellence in scholarship," which categorically includes internationalized scholarship, should remain the primary area of focus in tenure and promotion policies. Although senior administrative leaders at both institutions revealed that groups of faculty have advocated that specific interests, such as gender, environmental, and diversity issues, should receive special recognition in the institutional reward system, in order to provide a central area of focus and parity in academic advancement across disciplines, "excellence in scholarship" has been maintained as the primary factor by which faculty are evaluated in Duke and Richmond's tenure and promotion policies.

Yet, this analysis begs the following question: Are global perspectives included in tenure and promotion policies' definitions of "excellence in scholarship?" At neither Duke nor Richmond was excellence in scholarship clearly defined. Duke's faculty appointment, promotion, and tenure guidelines articulated that "Judgments of academic excellence are complex.... [and focus on] the candidate's performance, especially as a teacher and a scholar. Scholarly productivity must reflect a serious and sustained commitment to the life of scholarship" (Duke University Office of the Provost, 2007, p. 20) Although Richmond's tenure and promotion policies were decentralized by school, the only school to define scholarly excellence was Richmond's School of Law, which explained it as reflecting "depth of research, high standards of accuracy and creativity, precision in analysis, clarity in language and organization, and a spirit of healthy inquiry into the values and assumptions that underpin law and society" (University of Richmond Office of the Provost, 2001, para. 3). Thus, although scholarly excellence was the guiding criterion in tenure and promotion policies at both institutions, neither institution's policies clearly defined this term.

However, given senior faculty and administrators' insistence that scholarly excellence remain the sole criterion for tenure and promotion decisions and junior faculty members' preference for international scholarship to be explicitly included in the tenure and promotion policies, a clear definition of scholarly excellence that incorporates the value of global perspectives in order to develop complex understandings of their areas of expertise could address the concerns of both emergent camps. Just as Ernest Boyer (1990), former president of the Carnegie Foundation for the Advancement of Teaching, challenged higher education institutions to broaden traditional concepts of scholarship, so too is it important to broaden concepts of excellence in scholarship to include global perspectives in order to develop complex, comprehensive understandings of a given area of knowledge.

Organizational Practices Summary

Essentially, Duke and Richmond's organizational practices provided critical infrastructure, networks, and resources for faculty to engage in the implementation of their institutions' internationalization plans. Through the process of differential investment, a diversity of resources was provided for faculty to connect their institution's internationalization goals with their unique scholarly agendas. Through the communication channels provided by international centers and strategic electronic resources, faculty gained awareness of and access to resources with which they could internationalize their scholarship. As a result, Duke and Richmond's organizational practices provided foundational support for faculty to address the challenges to faculty engagement—lack of awareness and lack of disciplinary connections.

Organizational Principles

Certain organizational principles—accepted codes of conduct that guide faculty teaching, research, and service—served as facilitators of faculty engagement in internationalization at Duke and Richmond. At both universities, interdisciplinarity and coordination emerged as organizational principles that encouraged faculty to participate in international initiatives.

However, at Duke University, additional influential organizational principles included collaboration, customization, and entrepreneurship (see Table 18).

Table 18. Cross-Case Comparison of Organizational Principles Used to Develop Faculty Engagement in Internationalization

Organizational principles	Duke University	University of Richmond
Interdisciplinarity	X	X
Coordination	X	X
Collaboration	X	
Customization	X	
Entrepreneurship	X	

Interdisciplinarity

Through this study, interdisciplinarity emerged as a seminal organizational principle that facilitated faculty involvement in internationalization. Interdisciplinarity, a widely accepted code of conduct at Duke and Richmond, encouraged faculty at both institutions to engage in research and teaching across two or more academic disciplines, in order to develop a comprehensive understanding of a topic that may be too complex to be solved with the knowledge and methodologies of a single discipline.

In particular, at both institutions there were abundant symbols, incentives, and infrastructural support mechanisms (e.g., interdisciplinary centers, seminars, and grants) to encourage faculty to pursue scholarship at the intersections of disciplines. At Richmond, the first internationalization plan (1986) highlighted the importance of examining cross-disciplinary dimensions of international issues, which was achieved through the development of the faculty seminar abroad, international studies program, and Richmond Quest program. At Duke, the first internationalization plan (1995) advocated "furnishing multidisciplinary opportunities" (p. 16) for faculty to integrate international perspectives into their scholarship, which was accomplished through the creation of numerous international centers.

Consequentially, a value of interdisciplinarity prompted faculty who were "latent supporters" of internationalization (Goodwin & Nacht, 1983; Green & Olson, 2003) to examine their scholarship from not only cross-disciplinary but cross-cultural vantage points, so that they could develop as comprehensive an understanding of their subject areas as possible, and in so doing engage in their institutions' internationalization. As such, the pervasive principle of interdisciplinarity enabled Duke and Richmond to address the challenge found in previous studies (e.g., Bond, 2003; Ellingboe, 1998) that divisions between disciplines can preclude faculty engagement in internationalization.

Coordination

Although coordination was an organizational principle that emerged at both institutions, it did so with varying degrees of prominence. Coordination was highly prominent in Richmond's organizational culture, as advocated in its internationalization plans and operationalized primarily through the Office of International Education. This office has harmonized faculty international initiatives by coordinating cross-school international teaching and research opportunities, the faculty seminar abroad, guidelines for taking students abroad, and the faculty international education survey (University of Richmond Office of International Education, 2007b).

Coordination was less prominent, however, at Duke University as an organizational principle that affected faculty involvement in internationalization. Duke's international centers and international faculty database system did provide avenues for coordination of faculty international initiatives across schools and departments, although study participants and documentation did not suggest that it was a highly influential principle.

As such, coordination as an organizational principle varied in its significance at Duke and Richmond, predicated by their institutional size and structure. As discussed in the context section, Richmond's relatively smaller institutional size and centralized structure may have contributed to the prevalence of coordination as a principle that facilitated widespread faculty involvement in the implementation of the institution's internationalization plans. Accordingly, Richmond's composition of fewer faculty, schools, and acres enhanced the ability of its Office of International Education to harmonize faculty international initiatives through its coordination of cross-school international teaching and research initiatives and the faculty seminar abroad.

However, as Duke emerged as a more decentralized institution due to its larger size, coordination of faculty engagement in internationalization was achieved primarily through the institution's decentralized international and area studies centers, such as Duke's Asian/Pacific Studies Institute and Center for Latin American and Caribbean Studies, rather than Duke's central international office, the Office of the Vice Provost for International Affairs. Thus, the importance and channels of coordination differed at the two institutions investigated due to their institutional size and organizational structure.

Customization, Entrepreneurship, and Collaboration

Whereas coordination was prominent at Richmond, the principles of customization, entrepreneurship, and collaboration emerged as supportive of developing faculty engagement in internationalization plans at Duke.

Customization. Given Duke's larger size and more decentralized organization, there was increased importance for the institution to create infrastructure through which faculty were encouraged to customize their participation in the institution's internationalization plans based upon their departmental agendas. As faculty tend to prioritize their teaching and research based on the current needs and issues of their disciplines rather than their institutions, Duke's president and provost addressed this faculty tendency by requesting that each school develop an internationalization section in its own strategic plan. As a result, the institution's overarching goals for internationalization, as articulated in the university strategic plan and distinct document for internationalization, were customized to each discipline, which thereby created explicit connections to faculty scholarly interests.

Entrepreneurship. The principle of entrepreneurship has encouraged faculty to discover and pursue international initiatives that advance their teaching and research agendas. As a key part of Duke's first internationalization plan was to fuel the independent energies of faculty, Duke's internationalization has taken place in a highly entrepreneurial environment. In fact, because Duke is not located in a major metropolitan center, its geographic location has prompted faculty to bring the world into their research and classrooms. As advocated by Duke's strategic plan (2006) entrepreneurial activities by schools and institutes are valued. This value has translated into the "entrepreneurial spirit" of Duke's faculty. Combined with the customization of internationalization goals by discipline, the principle of entrepreneurship has served as a catalyst for faculty to explore international dimensions within their scholarly agendas.

Yet, it is possible that if the organizational principle of entrepreneurship continues to guide Duke faculty members' participation in international initiatives, these "lone cowboys" may advance their own scholarly agendas without advancing the goals of their institution's internationalization plans. As such, there is a fine balance between promoting independent and coordinated faculty activities. It is useful to note, however, that Duke's international faculty database serves as a mechanism in which faculty can post, share, and coordinate the international initiatives they have developed. Therefore, this analysis suggests that careful monitoring of the balance between Duke's entrepreneurial and coordinating organizational principles can help the institution avoid potential dangers of the scale tipped toward entrepreneurship, which could lead to the lone cowboy effect, and the scale tipped toward coordination, which could lead to the group think effect.

Collaboration. Collaboration emerged as a widely accepted principle at Duke that encouraged faculty to develop partnerships with colleagues within their institution (i.e., through the interdisciplinary centers and seminars focused on international topics), as well as colleagues at neighboring and international institutions (i.e., South Asian faculty seminars with North Carolina Central University and development of the medical campus overseas with the National University of Singapore), as a means through which to internationalize their scholarship.

Organizational Principles Summary

Organizational principles facilitated faculty engagement in internationalization through their provisions of accepted norms of conduct—interdisciplinarity, coordination, customization, entrepreneurship, and collaboration—that guided faculty involvement in international teaching, research, and service. In particular, interdisciplinarity was critical in breaking down cognitive barriers for Duke and Richmond faculty to pursue their scholarship from multiple disciplinary and cultural perspectives in order to gain a comprehensive understanding of the complex questions they are addressing in their teaching and research. Coordination emerged as a critical principle within Richmond's centralized organizational culture that streamlined and facilitated faculty involvement in internationalization. However, Duke's decentralized culture lent itself to the prevalence of customization, entrepreneurship, and collaboration to support faculty engagement in internationalization, which encouraged faculty to customize their engagement in internationalization based upon their departmental agendas, discover and pursue international initiatives that advance their personal scholarly agendas, and collaborate with colleagues within and outside the institution in order to advance their international scholarship.

Internationalization Plans

Duke and Richmond both integrated internationalization into their university strategic plans and created distinct documents for university-wide internationalization (see Table 19). However, Duke took the extra step of integrating internationalization into all nine of its school strategic plans. As such, the implementation of faculty engagement strategies at Duke and Richmond differed based on the centralization versus decentralization of the institutions' internationalization plans.

Table 19. Cross-Case Comparison of Internationalization Plan Types

Internationalization plan type	Duke University	University of Richmond
University Strategic Plan	X	
Distinct Document	X	X
Unit Plan	X	

Because Duke employed centralized and decentralized internationalization plans (i.e., university strategic plans, university-wide distinct documents for internationalization, and unit plans for internationalization), faculty engagement strategies were implemented at not only institutional levels, through infrastructural, programmatic, and financial support provided by central institutional offices, but also at individual subunit levels, through support provided by individual schools. This implementation of strategies at multiple organizational levels was particularly important given Duke's larger institutional size.

However, Richmond's strategies were implemented primarily through central institutional levels (i.e., through infrastructural, programmatic, and financial support provided by university strategic plans and university-wide distinct documents for internationalization) and allocated by centralized institutional offices (i.e., the Office of International Education).

Due to Richmond's smaller institutional size, this centralized implementation of faculty engagement strategies was appropriate and effective in encouraging widespread faculty involvement in the implementation of Richmond's internationalization plans. However, due to the larger institutional size and more diverse array of disciplines, the decentralization of implementation strategies at multiple institutional levels emerged as a facilitating factor in the development of widespread faculty participation in Duke's internationalization plans.

Alignment of Faculty Engagement Strategies in Internationalization Plans

Although both institutions had multiple internationalization plans, all 18 of Duke's faculty engagement strategies emerged in multiple plans, whereas three of Richmond's strategies emerged in more than one plan (see Table 20). Thus, the greater alignment of Duke's faculty engagement strategies promoted the infusion of internationalization support, in terms of symbols, finances, infrastructure, and programs, both broadly and deeply throughout the institution, which is critical to comprehensive internationalization (Engberg & Green, 2002; Green & Olson, 2003; Green & Shoenberg, 2006; Olson et al., 2005, 2006). Although there was a lesser degree of alignment among the strategies articulated in Richmond's internationalization plans, given Richmond's smaller institutional size, this lack of significant alignment was appropriate and did not preclude the broad, deep infusion of support for faculty engagement in internationalization throughout the institution.

Table 20. Cross-Case Analysis of Strategies Articulated in
Internationalization Plans

Strategy	Number of Duke's internationalization plans wherein strategy is articulated	Number of Richmond's internationalization plans wherein strategy is articulated
Overseas partnerships	10	-
Funding resources	7	2
International centers	7	1
Alignment with other university-wide initiatives	6	1
Departmental collaborations	5	1
Hiring	5	3
Faculty seminars	4	2
Internationally focused committees	4	1
Central international office	4	1
Support for distinguished international scholars	4	-
International conferences	3	-
International consulting	3	-
International degree programs	3	1
US partnerships	3	-
Support for faculty and school interests	3	-
Technology	3	-
Database	2	-
Recommended inclusion of international scholarship in tenure and promotion policies	2	1

Internationalization Plan Summary

In short, the development of all three types of internationalization plans at Duke emerged as important at Duke due to its large, decentralized characteristics. However, the development of two types of internationalization plans, both at the institutional level, emerged as sufficient at Richmond, considering its smaller, more centralized characteristics. As Duke's internationalization plans demonstrated greater alignment of faculty engagement strategies, this provided reinforcing support at multiple levels throughout the institution for faculty to engage in internationalization, which was particularly important given Duke's decentralized organization.

Chapter V

Implications and Conclusions

So, how has the development of faculty engagement affected the operationalization of internationalization plans at Duke University and University of Richmond? Both institutions' internationalization plans sought to advance the frontiers of knowledge and develop students' global competencies. Therefore, in the words of Duke's 2003 internationalization plan, the "sine qua non" (p. 15) of the implementation of internationalization plans was faculty engagement. For Duke and Richmond to avoid the SPOTS syndrome, or the tendency for institutional change documents to remain "Strategic Plans on the Shelf" (Parsons & Fidler, 2005; Piercy, 2002), it was critical to engage faculty in discussions of the desired internationalization goals for the institution, and develop strategies to enhance faculty members' knowledge, skills, and resources necessary to realize those goals.

Because faculty have direct authority and involvement in curricular content changes, Duke's reaccreditation process provided an avenue through which faculty could recognize the lack of cross-cultural emphasis in the core curriculum, discuss its importance, and make revisions to ensure students' development of cross-cultural competencies. Furthermore, as faculty have direct authority about whether to engage in international research collaborations, Duke and Richmond's interdisciplinary faculty seminars provided opportunities for faculty to discuss the benefits of exploring their research agendas from various disciplinary perspectives, which opened the doors to discussions and collaborations on research projects from various cultural and national perspectives to solve complex scholarly problems.

Finally, faculty who lack exposure to and involvement with different cultural perspectives may lack the knowledge, skills, and interest in engaging in internationalization. Yet, both Duke and Richmond provided resources and incentives for faculty to develop and act on an inclination to integrate cross-cultural perspectives into their teaching and research. For example, through Duke faculty members' participation in (a) interdisciplinary seminars through which they developed collaborative international research projects; (b) a reaccreditation process in which they discussed and revised the core curriculum to reflect the importance of cross-cultural competencies; and (c) pedagogical workshops with colleagues at neighboring institutions to share strategies for integrating international experiences into curricula, Duke faculty operationalized their institution's internationalization plans. The involvement of Richmond faculty was similarly critical in the realization of their institution's internationalization plan goals. Through Richmond faculty members' participation in the institution's "faculty seminars overseas" program, faculty encountered transformational experiences that prompted them to recognize on a personal and professional level the value of integrating international and cross-cultural perspectives into their pedagogy, curricula, and research.

Institutional Contexts

The contexts in which faculty have engaged in the operationalization of internationalization plans at the two institutions played critical roles in the development of faculty engagement. First, the large endowments of Duke and Richmond—$4.6 billion and $1.6 billion, respectively (Duke University Office of News and Communications, 2007; University of Richmond Advancement Office, 2007)—led to the development of significant financial resources with which faculty could pursue scholarship overseas and internationalize their curricula on campus. But large endowments alone would not have facilitated faculty engagement in internationalization. Rather, Duke and Richmond developed targeted funds to encourage and support faculty to participate in international teaching, research, and service initiatives.

Second, Duke's larger institutional size, in terms of acreage, schools, faculty and student populations, created a foundation for decentralized faculty engagement strategies, e.g., international and area studies centers and the integration of internationalization into each school's strategic plans, to encourage faculty across the institution to connect their individual scholarly agendas with the institution-wide plans for internationalization.

Third, senior institutional leaders, such as provosts at Richmond, and provosts, presidents, and the board of trustees at Duke, provided symbolic leadership (Bolman & Deal, 2003) to indicate the centrality of internationalization to the institutions' mission and allocated resources to support faculty engagement in operationalizing the internationalization plans. Fourth, Duke and Richmond developed their internationalization plans at multiple institutional levels, which provided reinforcement and prevalent messages about the importance and resources for faculty to engage in international scholarship. Both institutions integrated internationalization into the university strategic plans and developed distinct documents for internationalization. Additionally, at the request of the president and provost, all of Duke's nine schools integrated internationalization into their school strategic plans. Thus, through the symbolic, programmatic, and financial support provided by the various internationalization plans at each institution, faculty were prompted to see the importance of and the resources to take part in their institutions' internationalization.

Academic Activities

Academic activities, such as faculty seminars and international teaching opportunities prompted faculty involvement in internationalization. Most notably, faculty seminars functioned as seminal academic activities through which Duke and Richmond developed faculty engagement in international scholarship. Although both institutions' seminars were interdisciplinary in focus, they had significantly different forms. Duke's various types of seminars sponsored by different university centers took place on campus and gave faculty release time to focus on particular international themes with colleagues from a variety of disciplines.

Conversely, Richmond had a singular type of seminar that was run by a single institutional unit: Richmond's "faculty seminar abroad" program, administered by the Office of International Education, provided a centralized infrastructure through which a different group of faculty from various departments have convened every two years to study a world region for several weeks together on campus, followed by a three week group sojourn overseas to meet with national leaders, business people, academic colleagues, and local artisans to gain an understanding of the region. At both Duke and Richmond, their distinct seminars have similar outcomes: faculty participants' development of newly developed international curricula and collaborative international research grants.

In addition to faculty seminars, international teaching opportunities provided support for faculty to internationalize their curricula on campus and participate in teaching overseas. In particular, international degree programs created forums in which faculty were stimulated to explore international scholarship with students on the home campus, whereas Duke's medical campus overseas provided opportunities for faculty to engage in internationalizing their teaching and curricula. Although Richmond did not develop a campus abroad, by providing support for faculty to integrate study abroad into on-campus courses and to teach on summer study abroad programs, Richmond overcame a common obstacle to faculty participation in teaching overseas—lack of time (e.g., Burn, 1980; Engberg & Green, 2002; Morris, 1996).

Organizational Practices

Organizational practices also significantly influenced faculty engagement in internationalization. Specifically, both institutions made substantial investments in internationalization, e.g., international centers, seminars, curriculum integration grants, and international scholarship endowments, which created significant resources with which faculty were enabled to engage in international activities. Moreover, both institutions' use of strategic electronic resources served as communication channels through which faculty became informed of these resources.

Where the institutions diverged in their organizational practices is around the centralization or decentralization of international resources for faculty as an organizational practice. Although Duke has a centralized international office—the Office of the Vice Provost for International Affairs (OVPIA)—it was not this office as a whole, but rather the decentralized international centers (i.e., Asian Pacific Studies Institute, Center for Latin American and Caribbean Studies) that are under the OVPIA's purview, which emerged as strategic resources that directly affected faculty engagement in international activities. Conversely, at Richmond, the development of a centralized office—the Office of International Education—emerged as a critical structure that provided a foundation from which faculty throughout the institution engaged in international activities.

Organizational Principles

Moreover, prevalent organizational principles, i.e., interdisciplinarity, coordination, customization, entrepreneurship, and collaboration, affected faculty engagement in internationalization. At both universities, faculty members' value of interdisciplinarity created a foundation that stimulated their involvement in international teaching and research. As interdisciplinarity emphasizes comparative approaches, this organizational principle served as a launching pad for Duke and Richmond faculty to advance the complexity and comprehensiveness of their scholarship through the integration of cross-cultural perspectives.

Coordination was particularly prominent at Richmond, which may have been facilitated by its smaller institutional size and centralized structure. In particular, Richmond's Office of International Education coordinated international teaching and research opportunities for faculty of all disciplines, which provided a clear access point for faculty to gain information and resources to engage in internationalization. At Duke, instead of coordination, the principles of customization, entrepreneurship, and collaboration encouraged faculty to customize the institution-wide internationalization plans with their disciplinary priorities, initiate their own international initiatives, and collaborate with colleagues in departments throughout Duke, in local universities, and in institutions overseas to advance the internationalization of their scholarship.

Internationalization Plan Types

The implementation of each institution's faculty engagement strategies differed based upon the internationalization plan types employed. The greatest difference in strategy implementation emerged from the development of unit plans for internationalization, which took place at Duke and not at Richmond. Although Duke and Richmond both integrated internationalization into their university strategic plans and created distinct documents for internationalization, internationalization was also integrated into all nine of Duke's school strategic plans. Therefore, whereas Richmond's faculty engagement strategies were implemented through central institutional levels (i.e., the Office of International Education), Duke's strategies were implemented at both central institutional levels (i.e., the Office of the Vice Provost of International Affairs) and at individual subunit levels (i.e., individual schools).

The Five I's of Faculty Engagement in Internationalization

Faculty engagement in Duke and Richmond's internationalization has been comprised of a combination of five essential components, which are highlighted by the new model presented in this study. This model breaks down the process of faculty engagement in Duke and Richmond's internationalization into its constituent parts: (a) intentionality, (b) investments, (c) infrastructure, (d) institutional networks, and (e) individual support. Just as no one variable leads to internationalization in Knight's cycle, no one variable leads to faculty engagement in this cybernetic model (Birnbaum, 1988), which is replete with interactive subsystems. As a cybernetic model, this faculty engagement framework emphasizes the interconnectivity among institutional subsystems, feedback loops, and stakeholders, which was critical in Duke and Richmond's strategic development of faculty engagement in internationalization. As such, this model is visually depicted as a Venn diagram[13] that emphasizes the connections among each overlapping loop in Duke and Richmond's strategies to engage faculty in internationalization.

---

[13] Venn diagrams were developed originally by British philosopher and mathematician John Venn in 1880 as conceptual maps to demonstrate logical relationships within a theory (Venn, 1880).

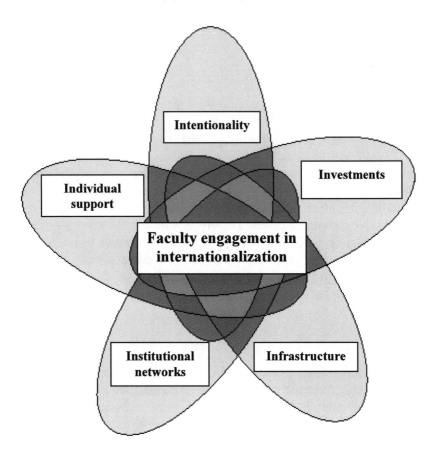

Figure 3. The five I's of faculty engagement in internationalization.

Intentionality

As with the overarching process of comprehensive internationalization (Olson et al., 2006), the embedded process of faculty engagement in internationalization also requires intentionality. The intentional development of faculty engagement in Duke and Richmond's internationalization was achieved through the creation of multiple types and levels of internationalization plans, which formalized internationalization as an institutional priority and provided focus, organization, and resources for faculty to engage in internationalization. Moreover, the "outrageous ambitions" advocated by Duke's former president Terry Sanford and the "dramatic gestures" and "iconic moments" emphasized by Richmond's dean of international education Uliana

Gabara intentionally promoted the engagement of faculty in their institutions' internationalization.

Investments

Duke and Richmond supported their faculty to engage in internationalization through investments from diverse sources (i.e., federal, private, and institutional) and at various locations throughout the institutions (i.e., central international offices, individual schools, individual interdisciplinary and area studies centers). For example, through the federal government's Title VI program, Duke has been able to provide grants for international research and conference attendance to faculty. Through endowed alumni funds, Richmond has been able to provide funds for faculty to conduct international research and service projects. Through institutional funds, both Duke and Richmond have provided faculty with financial support to internationalize existing and new curricula. These funds have been allocated through various institutional levels, i.e., Duke's Trinity College of Arts and Sciences, Duke's Office of the Vice Provost for International Affairs, Duke's Office of Study Abroad, Richmond's College of Arts and Sciences, and Richmond's Office of International Education. Richmond's Office of International Education has even offered to cover faculty members' passport application fees, as an example of their willingness to invest in faculty members' readiness to engage in international scholarly activities. As such, through the process of differential investment in their internationalization plans, Duke and Richmond have provided financial resources from a variety of sources, in a variety of increments, dispersed at a variety of locations throughout the institution (see Table 17 presented earlier), which thereby granted faculty financial support to engage in the implementation of their institutions' internationalization plans.

Infrastructure

Supportive infrastructure has served as the foundation for supplying Duke and Richmond faculty with organizational and programmatic resources through which to explore international perspectives within their teaching and research agendas. This infrastructure has included academic activities and organizational practices, such as faculty seminars, international degree programs, and a campus overseas. This infrastructure, which was largely international and interdisciplinary in nature, developed widespread faculty engagement in internationalization by providing opportunities to broaden and deepen relationships among faculty from various departments within the institution, at neighboring universities, and at institutions overseas.

Institutional Networks

As collaboration is a critical component of internationalization, institutional networks are essential to create the communication channels for faculty to learn about international opportunities, resources, and their colleagues' areas expertise and regional interests. Institutional networks, in varying degrees of institution-wide reach, included campus-wide internationalization committees, international faculty Web portals, international faculty seminars, and international centers. Campus-wide internationalization committees emerged as institutional networks that enabled committee members to share international resources and information. Surprisingly, these committees emerged as closed networks and this communication channel did not extend to faculty who were not committee members. Yet, the international faculty Web portal on Duke and Richmond's Web sites provided a centralized mechanism for faculty across campus to learn about opportunities and resources through which to engage in international teaching, research, and service (i.e., international research grants and curriculum internationalization grants). In particular, Duke's international faculty database system has provided a network through which faculty can independently develop research partnerships. Richmond's international education faculty survey and international academic travel guidelines enable the central Office of International Education to coordinate faculty international travel and connect faculty with relevant international opportunities based upon their scholarly expertise and regional interests.

Individual Support

Because the substance of internationalization—integration of international perspectives into teaching, research, and service—is carried out by individual faculty members, to operationalize Duke and Richmond's internationalization plans, it was necessary to provide support for faculty to connect institution-wide goals for internationalization with their individual scholarly agendas. Specifically, Duke's integration of internationalization into all nine schools' strategic plans provided links between internationalization and disciplinary priorities. Richmond's international education faculty survey enabled its Office of International Education to individually connect faculty members with international opportunities based upon their identified areas of expertise and regional interests.

Overview of Conceptual Model

Overall, this conceptual model presents major elements of Duke and Richmond's strategic development of faculty engagement in internationalization. This model emphasizes the importance of intentionally investing in and creating infrastructure for institutional networks and individual support to thrive, so that Duke and Richmond faculty have been encouraged to participate in the implementation of their institutions' internationalization plans. Furthermore, as demonstrated by this circular model, good things begot good things. In other words, both institutions developed internationalization plans in which they articulated their goals and priorities for internationalization. Both institutions then committed resources, developed infrastructure, enhanced their communication channels, and supported faculty to connect their individual scholarly agendas with the internationalization plans. In so doing, the internationalization efforts picked up momentum and encouraged faculty involvement. Through such an intentional process, internationalization not only became operationalized as an institutional focus, but as a focus that had benefits for faculty from diverse disciplines throughout the institution.

Typology of Strategies for Faculty Engagement in Internationalization

Various types of strategies implemented in various locations affected faculty engagement in Duke and Richmond's internationalization. To indicate this strategic development, the researcher has created a typology of strategies for faculty engagement in internationalization (see Tables 21 and 22). As this typology presents, three types of strategies—teaching, research, and service—took place in three different locations—on campus, off campus and regional, and off campus and abroad.

Table 21. Typology of Strategies for Faculty Engagement in
         Internationalization

Strategy type	Location
Teaching	On campus
Research	Off campus-regionally
Service	Off campus-abroad

As each strategy occurred and can occur in each different location, the typology, in fact, represents a total of nine distinct strategies for faculty engagement in internationalization, as indicated by the following list and explained by Table 22.

1. Teaching On Campus
2. Teaching Off Campus and Regionally
3. Teaching Off Campus and Abroad
4. Research On Campus
5. Research Off Campus and Regionally
6. Research Off Campus and Abroad
7. Service On Campus
8. Service Off Campus and Regionally
9. Service Off Campus and Abroad

Overview of Typology

This typology presents the major types of strategies and locations in which Duke and Richmond developed faculty engagement to promote the implementation of their internationalization plans. This typology indicates that although there are three overarching types of strategies and three overarching locations, there are, in fact, nine distinct, overarching strategies, when the strategy types and locations are combined, through which Duke and Richmond developed faculty participation in internationalization.

Implications for Practice

The emergent faculty engagement model and typology offer practical implications for institutional leaders seeking to develop faculty engagement in their institutions' internationalization plans. The implications for practice can be adapted based on unique institutional needs and are organized by the constituent parts of the faculty engagement model.

Intentionality

Just as an internationalization plan represents an intentional commitment to internationalizing an institution, it is similarly important for institutional leaders to develop intentional strategies to engage faculty in the operationalization of that plan. For institutional leaders seeking to advance this process, it will be important to ask the following questions: What are the goals and resources for faculty involvement in the implementation of an internationalization plan? What central units and subunits are responsible for overseeing, developing, and implementing support for faculty engagement in internationalization? These questions will help institutional leaders determine the type of faculty engagement, e.g., curricular reforms or research collaborations, needed to operationalize an internationalization plan, as well as the organizational mechanisms and resources available to support such faculty involvement.

Table 22. Explanation and Examples of Faculty Engagement
in Internationalization Typology

	Teaching	Research	Service
On Campus	Opportunities for faculty to internationalize their pedagogies and curricula. EX: Curriculum internationalization grants offered at Duke and Richmond for faculty to develop new and revise existing syllabi to integrate international perspectives into their curricula.	Opportunities for faculty to learn how to integrate their international experiences into their pedagogies and curricula. EX: Through the NC Center for South Asia Studies, Duke faculty have participated in teaching workshops with colleagues at regional institutions to share strategies on how to incorporate their South Asian experiences and backgrounds into their teaching.	Opportunities for faculty to teach at institutions in other countries. EX: Development of Duke's medical campus in Singapore international degree programs has created the infrastructure through which faculty have engaged in teaching overseas.
Off Campus-Regional	Opportunities for faculty to integrate international and cross-cultural perspectives into the scholarly agendas. EX: Through Duke's faculty seminars, faculty have been provided with teaching release time to participate in semester- or year-long residential seminars through which to develop interdisciplinary and international research partnerships.	Opportunities for faculty to develop international research partnerships with colleagues at local and regional institutions based on mutual disciplinary and regional interests. EX: Duke's Title VI area studies centers, i.e., the Consortium in Latin American & Caribbean Studies at the University of North Carolina at Chapel Hill and Duke University provide such international research partnerships.	Opportunities for faculty to develop partnerships with colleagues in other countries to conduct research. EX: Richmond's faculty seminar abroad, through which faculty interact with academic colleagues, government officials, and business people overseas, provides opportunities for faculty to make connections to develop research partnerships with colleagues overseas.
Off Campus-Abroad	Opportunities for faculty to engage in advising students on international matters and participate on campus internationalization committees. EX: By serving as study abroad and international service project advisors, Richmond and Duke faculty increased their on-campus communications with students and colleagues on international topics.	Opportunities for faculty to participate in cross-cultural service projects in the local and regional communities. EX: Richmond faculty received grant support to develop a program that promoted the integration of Mexican immigrants into the Richmond community.	Opportunities for faculty to participate in service endeavors overseas, by offering their expertise on pro bono projects in developing nations. EX: Duke medical faculty participated in service projects in Uganda, where they trained local surgeons on new equipment used for brain and spinal procedures.

After considering the connections between internationalization plan goals and faculty involvement, internationalization leaders should consider revisions to existing infrastructure and institutional networks to broaden and deepen faculty involvement in their institutions' internationalization.

If internationalization is articulated as a priority in the institution's strategic plan, internationalization leaders should charge an interdisciplinary group of faculty with developing a distinct internationalization plan, which articulates internationalization goals, resources, action items, targets, timelines, and strategies for faculty engagement. After that plan is presented and approved by senior institutional leaders, e.g., the president, provost, board of trustees, it is important for institutional leaders to assess whether it is appropriate to revise the existing group's charge or charge a new committee with overseeing the implementation of the plan. Otherwise, without concrete resource allocations and authority granted, the committee may not be able to effectively transition from the planning to implementation phases of developing faculty engagement in internationalization.

To promote the connection between internationalization plan goals and distinct disciplinary agendas, it is useful for an institution's president or provost to request and provide incentives for deans to integrate internationalization into their school's or department's strategic plans. As such, senior institutional leaders can intentionally promote the customization of internationalization goals with the diverse disciplines throughout the institution. This implication will be further discussed in the section on individual support.

Investments

To develop a strong financial foundation from which to support faculty engagement in international initiatives, internationalization leaders should assess current funding sources, types, and allocations that support faculty involvement in international initiatives. Are there additional sources of federal, state, local, private, and institutional funds (i.e., US Department of Education Title IV, president's and provost's office, interdisciplinary centers, school research committees, alumni donors) that could be solicited to develop faculty engagement in international teaching, research, and service? Because the institution has made a commitment to internationalization through the development of its internationalization plans, how might funds be reallocated internally to operationalize those plans?

The answers to these questions can help institutional leaders recognize opportunities and resources for differential investment in internationalization, which is the process of allocating and diversifying resources in various increments, types, and locations within an institution to develop the engagement of key stakeholders and, in so doing, operationalize the internationalization plans. By spreading the responsibility for funding faculty participation in international initiatives throughout the institution, institutional leaders can increase ownership and reinforce support for the operationalization of the plan.

In particular, institutions can advance faculty engagement in internationalization by incorporating international, transnational, and cross-cultural scholarship as priority funding areas in institution-wide and unit-wide research grant competitions. This prioritization would spread the responsibility for funding faculty involvement in international research among central institutional offices and academic subunits, as well as reinforce the importance of international research to the institution. Further, to ensure the long-term operationalization of an institution's internationalization plans, internationalization leaders should solicit financial support from a diversity of sources, such as those aforementioned, to create a global initiatives fund to support faculty member's international initiatives. This fund could provide seed grants for a limited period of time (e.g., one to two years) to get projects off the ground, after which time the responsibility for supporting such projects would shift to the departments, so that the responsibility for funding faculty member's international initiatives is shared between central institutional offices and disciplinary units. In addition to providing long-term support for faculty initiatives, the global initiatives fund could provide travel support for faculty to travel with colleagues or students for periods of time, ranging from one or two weeks to an entire semester, for courses or research overseas. Thus, a diversity of types and increments of financial resources can facilitate faculty participation in a variety of international initiatives, based upon individual faculty interests and commitments.

Infrastructure

Internationalization leaders should examine the current infrastructure in place to support faculty engagement in internationalization to ensure that faculty have relevant opportunities to internationalize their scholarship and service. *The following questions can help institutional leaders determine the necessary additions or revisions to programs that will enhance faculty participation in internationalization: What international centers, degree programs, seminars, institutional partnerships, and campuses exist that provide opportunities for faculty to engage and collaborate in international teaching, research, and service? Are the timing and locations of these resources conducive to faculty participation given faculty commitments? Are there deliver-*

ables such as producing internationalized syllabi or research projects that could be integrated into faculty members' participation in international seminars and programs? Making curricular or research integration deliverables a required component of faculty participation in such seminars and programs would provide structural mechanisms to ensure that faculty translate their international experiences, knowledge, and skills into their teaching and research.

Particularly as interdisciplinary centers and seminars provide support for faculty to explore cross-disciplinary and cross-cultural perspectives in their scholarship, it is important to consider in what ways interdisciplinary faculty programs can incorporate international dimensions. After assessing the existing infrastructural support in light of internationalization plan goals, it may be useful to augment the structural support to further promote faculty involvement in activities that will advance the institution's internationalization plans.

Moreover, chief international education administrators can use the faculty engagement typology (as presented earlier in Tables 21 and 22) to identify what kinds of international teaching, research, and service opportunities exist on the home campus, regionally, and abroad for faculty to participate in internationalization. As faculty who had "transformational experiences" overseas became immersed in their institutions' internationalization, it is particularly important to provide opportunities for faculty to engage in substantial teaching, research, or service endeavors abroad. This is so because professional experiences overseas enabled faculty to recognize the value of viewing themselves and their scholarly agendas through different cultural lenses. *By filling out Table 23, chief international education administrators can identify their institution's current strategies and discover opportunities for further development of faculty engagement in internationalization.*

Table 23. Types and Locations of Faculty Engagement Strategies

	On Campus	Off Campus-Regionally	Off Campus-Abroad
Teaching			
Research			
Service			

Institutional Networks

Internationalization leaders should identify and assess internal and external networks that promote faculty awareness of resources and participation in international initiatives, as communication channels are critical to faculty participation in internationalization (e.g., Aigner et al., 1992; Green & Olson, 2003; Harari, 1989). In addition to an institution's international centers and disciplinary departments, it is important for internationalization leaders to investigate opportunities for collaboration with neighboring and overseas institutions to maximize resources for faculty engagement. Just as Duke's Southeast Asian center created a partnership with its comparable center at North Carolina Central University so that faculty could share resources on curricular and research internationalization, partnerships among local institutions can enable institutions to multiply their resources for developing faculty knowledge and skills necessary to operationalize their internationalization plans.

Furthermore, particularly in this era of electronic communication, strategic and creative use of technologies can facilitate faculty awareness of and participation in international initiatives. For example, through electronic databases faculty can share international resources and projects; through electronic surveys central international offices can learn about the international interests and areas of expertise of faculty, through strategic e-mails chief international education administrators can inform faculty of opportunities to involve their international students or return study abroad students into classroom discussions; and through provision of videoconferencing institutional leaders can enable faculty virtually to bring international scholars and practitioners into their classrooms. *Therefore, it is important for internationalization leaders to consider the following questions: What electronic mechanisms, committees, and centers currently serve as communication channels through which faculty learn about and share international resources and opportunities?* Are there opportunities through strategic electronic communications that chief international education administrators can publicize statistics about the numbers of international students in their classes, study abroad students absent from their classes, and share suggested strategies to incorporate students' international perspectives into the classroom?

Institutional leaders may find it advantageous to streamline international resources for faculty in a central location on the institution's Web site and publicize this gateway, its location, and its benefits to faculty. By developing a central portal through which faculty can read the internationalization plan and learn about opportunities to participate in the implementation of this plan, faculty can gain awareness of and access to resources with which to connect their individual scholarly agendas with the internationalization plan. In addition, on this Web site, chief international education administrators could post a survey through which faculty can identify their experiences, interests, agendas, and regions of focus for international, teaching, research, and service. Through the information collected via this survey, chief international officers could target particular international resources and opportunities to particular faculty.

Moreover, on this Web site, internationalization leaders can create an electronic mechanism for faculty to share scholarly and regional interests and search for colleagues with mutual interests, in order to support development of joint research partnerships on international topics. By considering how communication networks can enable institutional centers to communicate international opportunities to faculty and for faculty to share international scholarly projects and regional interests, faculty engagement in the implementation of their institutions' internationalization can be promoted.

Duke and Richmond's internationalization committees served as useful networks for committee members to share information and resources for faculty involvement in international activities; however, these groups did not affect the involvement of the majority of faculty in the institution who were not committee members. This finding begs the following question: Does the committee have the authority and resources to oversee the implementation of the institution's internationalization plan? *In essence, the critical question is does the internationalization planning group have power?* Without power, this group cannot be effective in implementing the plan. Duke and Richmond's committees had power in the planning phase of Knight's (1994) internationalization cycle, but not in the operationalization phase. Therefore, these findings suggest that if a committee's charge has been limited to the development of an internationalization plan, it is essential that the charge is revised or a new group, such as an ongoing committee, is established and charged with overseeing the implementation of the plan. *For a committee to be effective in engaging faculty across campus, it must have high level status, similar to a faculty senate or faculty review committee, and have the power to make and follow through on decisions. As such, it would be useful for provosts who are interested in the operationalization of internationalization plans to create a faculty and senior administrator council, such as a council on international teaching and research, and charge this multidisciplinary group with designing and implementing strategies to support faculty engagement in internationalization.*

Individual Support

Fifth, it would be valuable for senior administrative leaders to evaluate the types and amount of support individual faculty are receiving to connect the institution's internationalization plan goals with their unique scholarly agendas. How can the support of individual schools, departments, and faculty be enhanced to engage faculty in the internationalization of their disciplinary goals, and thereby advance the implementation of their institution's internationalization plans? By considering how the institution is providing support for individual faculty to integrate international perspectives into their professional goals, interests, and projects, necessary additions and adjustments can be made to deepen faculty participation in internationalization.

For institutions with internationalization plans, it is useful for internationalization leaders to discuss with their presidents and provosts the value of requesting academic units to integrate internationalization into their individual unit strategic plans. In so doing, academic divisions can connect internationalization with their unique disciplinary priorities and, thereby, increase faculty engagement in the institution's internationalization goals.

Summary

This faculty engagement model can help institutional leaders develop faculty engagement in the operationalization of internationalization plans. In particular, this model highlights the importance of (a) intentionally creating internationalization plans and strategies for faculty engagement, (b) differentially investing in the implementation of those plans and strategies, (c) assessing and developing infrastructure (i.e., centers, seminars, programs, and resources) that supports faculty involvement, (d) assessing and developing institutional networks to provide communication channels for faculty engagement, and (e) assessing and developing support for faculty to connect their individual scholarly agendas with institutional goals for internationalization.

Implications for Institutional Change

Overall, this study offers implications for how institutions can operationalize institutional change agendas. As such, this section will highlight the necessity of networks to bridge individual agendas with institutional change agendas and the necessity to recognize and address loose coupling with institutions.

Necessity of Networks to Bridge Individual Agendas with Institutional Change Agendas

Stakeholder collaborations are essential to create desired transformational changes within an institution. *By increasing the contact faculty have with networks that support their development of knowledge, skills, and opportunities to participate in a given institutional change agenda, their engagement in the change agenda will likely increase. As such, networks inform stakeholders of opportunities, potential collaborations, and resources to participate in the change agenda, and in so doing, advance their individual agendas.* As there are both institutional and individual barriers to stakeholder participation in institutional change agendas (Bond, 2003; Green & Olson, 2003), networks provide the essential bridges to connect the interests and focuses of individual stakeholders with an institutional change agenda.

Necessity to Recognize and Address Loose Coupling within Institutions

Higher education institutions are composed of a series of loosely coupled, academic units that are responsive to each other, but retain separate identities and structures (Weick, 1976, 1982). Correspondingly, operationalizing an institutional change agenda is challenging, as individual units and stakeholders do not affect each other continuously, significantly, or directly (Eckel et al., 1999; Glassman, 1973; Orton & Weick, 1990; Weick, 1976).

Because wide-scale change in higher education institutions presupposes that stakeholders in units throughout the institution will alter the way they conceive of and carry out their primary teaching, research, and service activities (Eckel et al., 1999), creating feedback loops (Birnbaum, 1988) to promote interaction among loosely coupled units will prompt the collaboration and communication necessary to advance an institutional change agenda. Furthermore, individual stakeholders will be more likely to participate in an institutional change agenda if it is aligned with their intellectual foundations and interests. As such, the customization and integration of the institutional change agenda to individual unit priorities and contexts is critical to comprehensively transform an institution.

Universities, as loosely coupled institutions, are particularly prone to high-level initiatives that are not owned and, therefore, not implemented seriously by faculty. In loosely coupled institutions, in which faculty hold a great deal of autonomy over the execution of their professional responsibilities, it is important to develop mechanisms by which ownership is established by individual units to implement an institutional change initiative.

Therefore, *it is important to integrate institutional change priorities into not only institution-wide strategic plans, but also into unit strategic plans. This is critical because faculty carry out their professional responsibilities, i.e., teaching, research, and service, within the contexts of their disciplinary units.* Thus, the more that institutional goals are aligned with disciplinary priorities, the more faculty will become invested in the institutional change agenda.

Implications for Internationalization

In addition to the umbrella process of institutional change, this study offers implications for internationalization. Knight's (1994) internationalization cycle espouses that internationalization is comprised of six interconnected phases: (a) awareness, (b) commitment, (c) planning, (d) operationalization, (e) review, and (f) reinforcement. For institutions to proceed from the planning to operationalization stages of internationalization, faculty engagement is critical, as faculty are the stewards of an institution's teaching, research, and service. So, how can institutions bring internationalization to the epicenter of faculty activity? It is through the development of five foundational components: intentionality, investments, infrastructure, institutional networks, and individual support. Through the ongoing development and integration of these components, faculty engagement in an institution's internationalization agenda can be encouraged and facilitated.

To further shed light on how this model advances internationalization, implications will be discussed in the context of each component of the new faculty engagement model.

Intentionality

Just as intentionality should be a hallmark of institutional change in the academy (Eckel, Hill, & Green, 1998), so too must intentionality be a cornerstone of internationalization. *Charting a deliberate plan that is congruent with institutional aspirations for internationalization and strategies to engage faculty to realize those aspirations is critical.* As such, it is critical for internationalization leaders to recognize the changes in faculty activities and focus required to operationalize their internationalization plans.

Strategic planning scholars (Parsons & Fidler, 2005; Piercy, 2002) have warned of the SPOTS syndrome, which is the tendency for well-intentioned institutional change documents to remain "Strategic Plans on the Shelf." To avoid the SPOTS syndrome, it is critical to engage faculty in discussions of the desired internationalization goals for the institution, as well as the faculty knowledge, skills, and resources that are necessary to realize those goals.

Investments

Resource dependence theory illuminates that individuals and institutions are dependent upon resources to implement their goals (Dooris & Lozier, 1990). Therefore, the operationalization of internationalization plans requires realistic investments of time and money. Yet, the tendency exists for internationalization to become yet another undervalued, underfunded initiative, which precludes faculty involvement in internationalization (Bond, 2003; Ellingboe 1998). Through the process of differential investment, Duke and Richmond demonstrated that it is possible to strategically allocate various types and amounts of financial resources throughout the institution, so that ownership and implementation of strategies to engage faculty in internationalization are dispersed in all corners of the institution. *How and where funds are dispersed throughout the institution is more influential than how many funds are dispersed. Thus, if funds are allocated at a variety of institutional levels, including through the offices of senior institutional leaders (e.g., offices of the president and provost), chief international education administrators, individual centers (i.e., international, area studies, and interdisciplinary centers), and individual schools or departments, the importance and support for faculty engagement in internationalization is reinforced throughout the institution.*

Furthermore, this study confirms the contentions of institutional change and internationalization scholars that even relatively small financial grants can yield significant benefits (Eckel et al., 1999; Green & Olson, 2003). For example, stipends of $1,500 for curricular integration at Richmond or $750 for international travel at Duke energized faculty to engage in the operationalization of their institutions' internationalization plans. By developing funds to support faculty engagement in internationalization through differential investment, institutions can multiply the development and operationalization of their resources.

Infrastructure

Infrastructural support for faculty engagement in internationalization supplies faculty with the organizational and programmatic resources through which to explore international perspectives within their teaching and research agendas. Faculty need infrastructural support to engage in internationalization, such as (a) adequate time to prepare course modifications, including release time during the academic year or time off during the summer and (b) sufficient resource materials in libraries (Backman, 1984; Carter, 1992; Johnston & Edelstein, 1993). Because these requirements for faculty involvement in internationalization suggest that widespread faculty support of internationalization is not endogenous, Duke and Richmond's development of structural support strategies addressed these challenges. For example, Duke's residential seminars provided release time—a prized faculty resource—to develop interdisciplinary connections and international research projects. The strategic organization of Richmond's faculty seminars included a newly developed reference section in the library that included faculty-participant selected readings on various disciplinary perspectives on the countries to be visited on the seminar. As Richmond's faculty seminars have taken place biennially during the summer over a period of three weeks, the institution has carved out time for faculty to explore international dimensions of their fields, without impeding on their teaching obligations. This is particularly important due to the burden placed on institutions to fill teaching vacancies on the home campus when faculty pursue teaching and research overseas (Ellingboe, 1998). Yet, by structuring opportunities for faculty to integrate short-term study abroad courses into on-campus, semester-long courses, Richmond demonstrated a creative infrastructural solution to this challenge.

For higher education institutions interested in operationalizing internationalization plans, it is important to provide structured opportunities for faculty to step out of their own disciplinary or cultural contexts and engage the issues with each other. Whether faculty step into another context far away from campus, as was done in Richmond's faculty seminars abroad, or into another space on campus, as was done in Duke's residential interdisciplinary seminars, it is critical to provide opportunities for faculty to challenge each other's thinking and thereby engage in internationalization.

Institutional Networks

Institutional networks provide the communication channels necessary for faculty to learn about international opportunities, resources, and their colleagues areas of international expertise and regional interests. Moreover, institutional networks serve specific functions that enhance faculty engagement in internationalization: Institutional networks (a) provide intellectual support and (b) create collaborative alliances that encourage faculty to incorporate international dimensions into their scholarship. As collaborative alliances are essential for institutional change (Kanter, 2000), the frequent, intensive communication among faculty from diverse disciplines prompted by in-person and virtual networks facilitates connections through which faculty can create international teaching and research partnerships to advance their scholarly agendas and their institution's internationalization plans. Thus, by promoting faculty connections on international themes, institutional networks can overcome the system of delayed and unclear feedback that is prevalent in loosely coupled organizations, and provide support for faculty to engage in the operationalization of their institution's internationalization plans.

Particularly in the current era of electronic communication, strategic use and organization of technologies can support the development of user-friendly institutional networks through which faculty become informed, share resources, and participate in international opportunities that advance their scholarly agendas and their institution's internationalization plans. Databases, Web sites, and blogs can enable the communication of international opportunities back and forth between international administrators and faculty, as well as the communication of international resources among faculty. For example, an institution can create an international faculty database system to enable faculty to search for colleagues engaged in world regions or research topics of interest, so that they can coordinate their scholarly initiatives. Or, an institution can create a centralized Web site to provide a comprehensive set of guidelines and resources for faculty engagement in international activities.

In addition to networks provided by electronic mechanisms, faculty seminars provide useful networks to connect faculty with colleagues from diverse disciplinary and cultural vantage points to augment the richness of their scholarly agendas. Faculty engagement in internationalization comes from not only what faculty know in terms of the international dimensions of their disciplines, but who they know. This is particularly important, as faculty need specific knowledge, skills, and attitudes to engage in international scholarship. Principally, seminars provide structured opportunities for faculty to (a) carve out time to focus on a particular internationalization theme, (b) engage in dynamic discussions about the theme with colleagues, (c) examine the theme from various disciplinary perspectives, and, in so doing, (d) develop critical knowledge, insights, and skills to overcome cognitive barriers (Ellingboe, 1998) that preclude faculty from internationalizing their scholarship.

Given the interdisciplinary nature of the networks that supported faculty engagement in internationalization, an institution with an ethos of interdisciplinarity is at an advantage to develop a foundation through which faculty engage in internationalization. In essence, an international mind-set (Paige & Mestenhauser, 1999) can be facilitated through an interdisciplinary mind-set. As Paige and Mestenhauser emphasized, to develop an international mind-set, it is critical for faculty to synthesize, connect, and integrate knowledge from diverse settings. As interdisciplinary approaches train faculty in transferring concepts between disciplines to advance their scholarship, interdisciplinarity creates a springboard for faculty to recognize and incorporate the benefits of integrating various cultural perspectives in order to generate new understandings of complex scholarly problems.

Overall, faculty require a dense web of interpersonal connections on a variety of disciplinary, interdisciplinary, and cultural levels to enhance their access to opportunities to internationalize their scholarship, and in so doing, advance the implementation of their institution's internationalization plans.

Individual Support

Disciplinary departments serve as the epicenter of faculty involvement. Given faculty member's primary allegiance to their departments, the prevalent faculty desire for autonomy, and the tendency for academic departments to operate independently from one another, individual support is just as critical to promoting collaborations through networks and seminars. But, what is meant by individual support? Individual support refers to strategies that connect institution-wide goals for internationalization with individual department and faculty agendas. This is particularly important, as how an institution's internationalization plan goals will be operationalized in, for example, a college of arts and sciences, will be different from a college of law. *Therefore, the development of deliberate strategies designed to align institutional plans for internationalization with unique disciplinary priorities is critical to developing widespread faculty engagement in internationalization.* Incentives, such as targeted funding resources and time off to develop research projects provide support for faculty to connect their individual scholarly agendas with institutional plans for internationalization.

Individual support provided by unit plans for internationalization enables institutions to address Weick's (1976) suggestion of the importance of localized adaptation in loosely coupled organizations. *Specifically, unit plans for internationalization provide opportunities for institutions to engage in localized adaptation.* Through each unit's integration of the internationalization plan goals into their individual unit strategic plans, internationalization is adapted to localized and specific disciplinary priorities. Thus, individual support, such as that provided by unit plans for internationalization, is essential to connect faculty from all disciplines with the institution's internationalization goals. Moreover, it is important for senior administrative leaders, e.g., provosts or chief international education administrators, to request departments to report on an annual basis how they have addressed their internationalization goals, so that these goals are not side-stepped or funded insufficiently by unit resources.

Figure 4. Nine Recommendations to Engage Faculty in Internationalization

The results of this study have led to the following nine recommendations to guide institutional leaders and scholars in developing faculty engagement in internationalization:

1. Differentially investing and allocating targeted resources at various institutional levels, e.g., through provost's offices, international and area studies centers, and individual schools, increases the likelihood of developing widespread faculty engagement in international scholarship.

2. For faculty to invest themselves in operationalizing a plan for institutional transformation, e.g., internationalization, faculty must encounter transformational change experiences on an individual level, so that their attitudes, beliefs and agendas become aligned with the institutional change agenda.

3. Faculty seminars can promote the development of the cognitive skills, awareness, and transformation necessary for faculty to become champions and advocates for their institution's internationalization.

4. After an internationalization plan has been developed, a senior administrative leader must charge a high level, interdisciplinary group of faculty and administrators with the authority and resources to oversee the implementation of the internationalization plan.

5. Student demand is an important factor in encouraging faculty to internationalize their curricula.

6. The incorporation of global perspectives into tenure and promotion policies' definition of "excellence in scholarship" can promote faculty engagement in internationalization.

7. A value of interdisciplinarity can provide a foundation for faculty to incorporate not only multiple disciplinary but also various national and cultural perspectives into their teaching and research agendas to develop a more comprehensive understanding of their scholarship.

8. The integration of internationalization into the strategic plans of individual academic units, i.e., schools or departments, augments faculty engagement by linking institution-wide plans for internationalization with distinct disciplinary priorities.

9. The main goal of faculty engagement strategies is to help faculty overcome endogenous obstacles to institutional change and to internationalization, which include lack of time, lack of financial resources, and disciplinary silos.

Ultimately, faculty must value internationalization on a personal level in order to become ardent supporters of the implementation of their institution's internationalization plans. Transformational experiences help faculty to become personally invested in an internationalization plan. Providing opportunities for faculty to have transformational experiences through which to recognize the value of examining a topic from different cultural or national perspectives is critical to developing the support of faculty who are not already champions or advocates of internationalization. In essence, transformational experiences are critical to connect individual concerns with internationalization.

Conclusion

Higher education institutions can bring to life their internationalization plans by strategically engaging faculty through the integration of five key components: intentionality, investments, infrastructure, institutional networks, and individual support. In essence, colleges and universities seeking to internationalize should intentionally articulate their internationalization goals, make long-term investments to provide resources targeted for faculty engagement, develop infrastructure to create foundational programmatic support, develop institutional networks to enable faculty to gain awareness of international opportunities, and provide support for individual faculty to connect institutional goals for internationalization with their personal scholarly agendas.

Overall, it is important to provide opportunities for faculty to develop the awareness of, capacity for, and community around internationalizing their teaching, research, and service both on and off campus. Faculty need the inclination, as well as the skills and knowledge, to internationalize their scholarship. To operationalize these objectives, specific academic activities, organizational practices, and organizational principles need to encourage faculty to engage in a lively exchange to connect the disciplinary topics they cared about with their institution's internationalization agenda. In particular, the interdisciplinary seminars can provide structured opportunities for faculty to cross disciplinary boundaries, and in so doing open their eyes to the benefits of crossing national and cultural boundaries in their scholarship. Through such collaborative efforts at various institutional and subunit levels, universities and colleges can support faculty to internationalize their curricula, pedagogy, and research, through creating alliances and marshalling resources to facilitate faculty involvement.

Ultimately, the "Five I's of Faculty Engagement" and "Typology for Faculty Engagement in Internationalization" present a compass that can guide the involvement of faculty, so that institutions' internationalization plans are not confined to bookshelves or filing cabinets, but infiltrated class-rooms and research agendas, thereby broadening the international under-standing of all students and faculty.

Appendix

Methodology

A qualitative, multiple-case study was selected as the research design for this study to shed light on a poorly understood phenomenon and discover thus far unspecified contextual variables. A multiple-case study design enabled the researcher to (a) understand the complexities of each case and (b) identify components that can be compared and contrasted across cases. By addressing the same research question in multiple settings and using the same data collection and analysis procedures, this design allowed the researcher to consciously seek cross-site comparison without necessarily sacrificing within-site understanding.

Table 24. Sampling Methods

Sampling method	Description
Expert-driven	Expert-driven sampling involved consulting with internationalization expert Madeleine Green, ACE vice president, for a previous study the researcher conducted with ACE. Green selected 2 out of 194 total AIEA-member institutions, based upon knowledge of their internationalization efforts and participation in ACE's internationalization programs.
Maximum variation	Maximum variation sampling was employed for the current study to select 2 institutions from the 31 responding institutions that collectively represented all three types of internationalization plans, based upon an internationalization plan typology, which the researcher developed in a previous study (Childress, 2009) conducted with ACE and included (a) institutional strategic plans, (b) distinct documents, and (c) unit plans for internationalization.
Criterion-based	Criterion-based sampling was used to select institutions that had internationalization committees and plans. Among the 31 responding institutions, 18 institutions had such committees. Among those 18 institutions, five institutions had internationalization plans. Thus, 5 institutions in total met the criteria for inclusion in the study. After invitations were extended to all five institutions to participate in the study, two universities accepted the invitation. These institutions were Duke University and University of Richmond, which collectively represented all three types of internationalization plans on the internationalization plan typology.

Population and Sampling Strategy

The population for this study included the 194 institutional members of the Association of International Education Administrators (AIEA). AIEA was selected as the population for investigation in this study, due to these institutions' demonstrated commitment to internationalization through their AIEA membership. Expert-driven, maximum variation, and criterion-based sampling methods comprised the sampling strategy for this study (see Table 24).

Data Collection

Data collection methods included document analysis, interviews, and focus groups. During document analysis, the researcher reviewed internationalization plans and related documents, e.g., internationalization committee charges, meeting minutes, agendas, reports; mission statements, capital campaign case statements; institutional leader speeches; and tenure, promotion, and hiring policies. The researcher triangulated data obtained in document analysis through interviews and focus groups.

Interviews were conducted with the AIEA representatives and two non-committee senior administrative leaders at each of the two institutions examined in this study. Focus groups were conducted with internationalization committee members at each of the two institutions examined in this study. The strength of interviews and focus groups in providing in-depth insights into the perspectives of key actors in the phenomenon under investigation complemented the strength of documents in their provision of exact details. The weakness of focus groups in terms of participants' potential political concerns about how their perspectives might be perceived by fellow group members was compensated for through the use of one-on-one interviews. Overall, multiple methods of data collection allowed the researcher to triangulate to maximize the strengths and minimize the limitations of each.

Data Analysis

The constant comparative method served as the primary analytical method used to systematically and continually categorize, compare, synthesize, and interpret the data collected . Particular to multiple-case studies, two stages of data analysis were involved: within-case and cross-case analysis (Merriam, 1998).

Within-case analysis. In the within-case analysis phase, the researcher examined the data of each individual case. Data were gathered so that the researcher could learn as much about the contextual variables affecting each case. After each document was imported into the qualitative data analysis software MAXqda, codes were assigned to segments of text based upon similar key words, phrases, and issues identified in the documents. In first-level coding, the researcher identified codes for emergent themes and text segments that relate to each code. As much as possible, the researcher used "in vivo" codes, which are codes that reflect participants' actual wording. In second-level coding, the researcher conducted pattern coding in order to group initial codes into a smaller number of themes (Merriam, 1998). Pattern coding was particularly important for this multiple-case study, as it led to the development of key themes, which laid the groundwork for cross-case analysis.

Cross-case analysis. In the cross-case analysis phase, abstractions were built across cases to generate a theory that fit the cases examined, although the cases varied in individual details (Merriam, 1998; Yin, 1994). To analyze data across cases, the researcher first relied upon the data collected and organized in the within-case analysis. By conducting "pattern clarification," comparisons and contrasts across the two cases were generated. Conceptually clustered matrices were employed in order to further clarify patterns and draw conclusions across cases. Such matrices enabled the researcher to organize and analyze convergent and divergent findings.

To ensure that emergent findings matched reality and to further enhance the credibility and dependability of the study, the researcher engaged in member checks through follow-up interviews with key participants at each institution. Through this process, participants assisted the researcher in fine-tuning her interpretations to better capture their perspectives, and in so doing, further establish the credibility and dependability of the findings.

Bibliography

Aigner, J. S., Nelson, P., & Stimpfl, J. (1992). Internationalizing the university: Making it work. Springfield, VA: CBIS Federal.

Alliance for International Educational and Cultural Exchange, & NAFSA: Association of International Educators. (2006). An international education policy for US leadership, competitiveness, and security. Retrieved November 16, 2006, from http://www.nafsa. org/_/Document/_/toward_an_international_1.pdf

Altbach, P. (2002). Perspectives on internationalizing higher education. International Higher Education. Retrieved November 6, 2006, from http://www.bc.edu/bc_org/avp/soe/cihe/ newsletter/News27/text004.htm

Altbach, P. (2006). What's in a name? Academe, 92(1), 48-49.

Armstrong, M. A., & Brown, D. (2006). Strategic reward: Making it happen. London: Kogan Page.

Association of American Colleges. (1985). Integrity of the college curriculum: A report to the academic community. Washington, DC: Association of American Colleges.

Association of American Universities. (2006). A national defense education act for the 21st century: Renewing our commitment to US students, science, scholarship, and security. Retrieved December 15, 2006, from http://www.aau.edu/education/NDEAOP.pdf

Association of International Education Administrators. (1995). Guidelines for international education at US colleges and universities. Washington, DC: Association of International Education Administrators.

Association of International Education Administrators. (2009). Mission. Retrieved April, 2006, from http://www.aieaworld.org/aboutus/mission.php

Back, K., Davis, D., & Olsen, A. (1996). Internationalisation and higher education: Goals and strategies. Canberra, Australia: Australian Government Publishing Service.

Backman, E. L. (1981). The development of an international commitment: A case study. Occasional Paper Series in International Education, 1(1), 3-17.

Backman, E. L. (Ed.). (1984). Approaches to international education. New York: Macmillan.

Bean, J. P., & Kuh, G. (1984). A typology of planning programs. Journal of Higher Education, 55(1), 35-55.

Beltos, N. J. (1988). Problems in defining the direction and content of international education for the 21st century. Ypsilanti, MI: Eastern Michigan University. (ERIC Document Reproduction Service No. ED304895).

Biddle, S. (2002). Internationalization: Rhetoric or reality? (No. ACLS Occasional Paper, No. 56). New York: American Council of Learned Societies.

Birnbaum, R. (1988). How colleges works. San Francisco: Jossey-Bass.

Bolinger, J. G. (1990). Strategic planning in an academic environment. Engineering Education, 80(1), 19-22.

Bond, S. (2003). Untapped resources: Internationalization of the curriculum and classroom experience. Canadian Bureau for International Education Research, 7, 1-15.

Bond, S., Qian, J., & Huang, J. (2003). The role of faculty in internationalizing the undergraduate curriculum and classroom experience. Canadian Bureau of International Education Research, 8, 1-20.

Bowman, K. (1990). A strategy for internationalization: The University of Oregon. International Education Forum, 10(1), 9.

Boyer, E. L., Altbach, P., & Whitelaw, M. J. (1994). The academic profession: An international perspective. Princeton, N.J.: The Carnegie Foundation for the Advancement of Teaching.

Brecht, R. D., & Walton, R. (2001). National language needs and capacities. In P. O'Meara, H. D. Mehlinger & R. M. A. Newman (Eds.), Changing perspectives on international education (pp. 103-138). Bloomington, IN: Indiana University Press.

Bremer, L., & van der Wende, M. (1995). Internationalizing the curriculum in higher education: Experiences in the Netherlands. The Hague, the Netherlands: Nuffic: Netherlands Organization for International Cooperation in Higher Education.

Brown, D. (2001). Reward strategies: From intent to impact. London: Chartered Institute of Personnel and Development.

Burn, B. B. (1980). Expanding the international dimension of higher education. San Francisco: Jossey-Bass.

Calof, J. C., & Beamish, P. (1995). Adapting to foreign markets: Explaining internationalization. International Business Review, 4(2), 115-131.

Canary, H. W., Jr. (1992). Linking strategic plans with budgets. Government Finance Review, 8(2), 21-24.

Carter, H. (1992). Implementation of international competence strategies: Faculty. In C. B. Klasek (Ed.), Bridges to the future: Strategies for internationalizing higher education (pp. 191-203). Carbondale, IL: Association of International Education Administrators.

Chandler, A. (1999). Paying the bill for international education: Programs, partners and possibilities at the millennium. Washington, DC: NAFSA: Association of International Educators.

Childress, L. (2009). Internationalization plans for American higher education institutions: The development and monitoring of written commitments to internationalization. Journal of Studies in International Education, 13(1), 289-309.

Cleveland-Jones, M., Emes, C., & Ellard, J. H. (2001). On being a social change agent in a reluctant collegial environment. Planning for higher education, 29(4), 25-33.

Cogan, J. (1998). Internationalization through networking and curricular infusion. In J. Mestenhauser & B. Ellingboe (Eds.), Reforming higher education curriculum: Internationalizing the campus (pp. 106-117). Phoenix, AZ: Oryx Press.

Collins, N. F., & Davidson, D. E. (2002). From the margin to the mainstream: Innovative approaches to internationalizing education for a new century. Change, 34(5), 50-58.

Commission on the Abraham Lincoln Study Abroad Fellowship Program. (2005). Global competence and national needs: One million American studying abroad. Retrieved January 29, 2006 from http:// www.lincolncommission.org/LincolnReport.pdf

Committee on the University and World Affairs. (1960). The university and world affairs. New York: Ford Foundation.

de Wit, H. (2002). Internationalization of higher education in the United States of America and Europe: A historical, comparative, and conceptual analysis. Westport, CT: Greenwood Press.

Deardorff, D. K. (2006). Identification and assessment of intercultural competence as a student outcome of internationalization. Journal of Studies in International Education, 10(3), 191-193.

Deutsch, S. E. (1970). International education and exchange: A sociological analysis. Cleveland, OH: The Press of Case Western Reserve University.

Dill, D. D., & Helm, K. P. (1988). Faculty participation in strategic policy making. In J. C. Smart (Ed.), Higher education: Handbook of theory and research: Vol. 4. New York: Agathon.

Dooris, M. J., Kelley, J. M., & Trainer, J. F. (2002). Strategic planning in higher education. In M. J. Dooris, J. M. Kelley, & J. F. Trainer (Eds.), Successful strategic planning (pp. 5-11). San Francisco: Jossey-Bass.

Dooris, M. J., & Lozier, G. (1990). Adapting formal planning approaches: The Pennsylvania State University. In F. A. Schmidtlein & T. H. Milton (Eds.), Adapting strategic planning to campus realities (pp. 83-93). San Francisco: Jossey-Bass.

Eckel, P., Hill, B., & Green, M. (1998). On change: En route to transformation. Washington DC: American Council on Education.

Eckel, P., Hill, B., Green, M., & Mallon, M. (1999). Reports from the road: Insights on institutional change. Washington, DC: American Council on Education.

Education and World Affairs. (1965). The university looks abroad: Approaches to world affairs at six American universities. New York: Walker and Company.

Egge, S. A. (1999). Creating an environment of mutual respect within the multicultural workplace both at home and globally. Management Decision, 37(1), 24-28.

Ellingboe, B. J. (1998). Divisional strategies to internationalize a campus portrait. In J. A. Mestenhauser & B. A. Ellingboe (Eds.), Reforming the higher education curriculum: Internationalizing the campus (pp. 198-228). Phoenix, AZ: The Oryx Press.

Ellingboe, B. J. (1999). Internationalizing the private liberal arts college: A comparative, five-college case study of components, strategies, and recommendations. Dissertation Abstracts International, 60(01), 77A. (UMI No. 9916427).

Engberg, D., & Green, M. F. (2002). Promising practices: Spotlighting excellence in comprehensive internationalization. Washington, DC: American Council on Education.

Fox, J. W. (1993). Economic and social challenges: New educational paradigms and needed attitude changes. Synthesis, 3(2), 10.

Francis, A. (1993). Facing the future: The internationalization of post-secondary institutions in British Columbia. Vancouver, Canada: British Columbia Centre for International Education.

Freedman, K. (1998). Culture in curriculum: Internationalizing learning by design. In J. Mestenhauser & B. Ellingboe (Eds.), Reforming the higher education curriculum: Internationalizing the campus. Phoenix, AZ: American Council on Education and Oryx Press.

Friedman, T. (2000). The Lexus and the olive tree: Understanding globalization. New York: Farrar, Straus, and Giroux.

Friedman, T. (2005). The world is flat: A brief history of the twenty-first century. New York: Farrar, Straus, and Giroux.

Gilliom, M. E. (1993). Mobilizing teacher educators to support global education in preservice programs. Theory into Practice, 32(1), 40-46.

Glassman, R. B. (1973). Persistence and loose coupling in living systems. Behavioral Science, 18,83-98.

Goodwin, C. D., & Nacht, M. (1983). Absence of decision: Foreign students in American colleges and universities. New York: Institute of International Education.

Goodwin, C. D., & Nacht, M. (1988). Abroad and beyond: Patterns in American overseas education. New York: Cambridge University Press.

Government Accountability Office. (2007). Global competitiveness: Implications for the nation's higher education system. Retrieved January 25, 2007, from http://www.gao.gov/new.items/d07135sp.pdf

Gray, A. W. (1977). International/intercultural education in selected state colleges and universities: An overview and five cases. Washington, DC: American Association of State Colleges and Universities.

Green, M. F. (2002). Joining the world: The challenge of internationalizing undergraduate education. Change Magazine, 34,(3), 13-21.

Green, M. F. (2003a, January). The challenge of internationalizing undergraduate education: Global learning for all. Paper presented at the Duke University's Global Challenges and US Higher Education Conference, Durham, NC.

Green, M. F. (2003b). Foreward. In R. F. Scherer, S. T. Beaton, M. F. Ainina & J. F. Meyer (Eds.), Internationalizing the business curriculum: A field guide (2nd ed., pp. xi-xiv). Euclid, OH: Williams Custom Publishing.

Green, M. F. (2003c). Internationalizing the campus: A strategic approach. International Educator, 7(1), 13-26.

Green, M. F. (2005a). Internationalization in US higher education: The student perspective. Washington, DC: American Council on Education.

Green, M. F. (2005). Measuring internationalization at research universities. Washington, DC: American Council on Education.

Green, M. F., & Olson, C. L. (2003). Internationalizing the campus: A user's guide. Washington, DC: American Council on Education.

Green, M. F., & Shoenberg, R. (2006). Where faculty live: Internationalizing the disciplines. Washington, DC: American Council on Education.

Groennings, S., & Wiley, D. (Eds.). (1990). Group portrait: Internationalizing the disciplines. New York: The American Forum.

Gutek, G. L. (1993). American education in a global society: Internationalizing teacher education. New York: Longman.

Harari, M. (1981). Internationalizing the curriculum and the campus: Guidelines for AASCU institutions. Washington, DC: American Association of State Colleges and Universities.

Harari, M. (1989). Internationalization of higher education: Effecting institutional change in The curriculum and campus. Long Beach: Center for International Education, California State University.

Harari, M. (1992). The internationalization of the curriculum. In C. B. Klasek (Ed.), Bridges to the future: Strategies for internationalizing higher education (pp. 52-79). Carbondale, IL: Association of International Education Administrators.

Hayward, F. M. (2000). Internationalization of US higher education: Preliminary status report. Washington, DC: American Council on Education.

Herzberg, F. (2003). One more time: How do you motivate employees? Harvard Business Review, 81(1), 87-96.

Institute for International Education. (2005). Open doors 2005: International students in the US Retrieved December 6, 2005, from http://opendoors.iienetwork.org/?p=69736

Institute for International Education. (2006). Economic impact of international students. Retrieved January 29, 2007 from http://opendoors.iienetwork.org/?p=92310

James, S., & Nef, J. (2002). Institutional factors in the internationalization of higher education. In S. Bond & C. Bowery (Eds.), Connections and complexities: The internationalization of higher education in Canada (pp. 126-148). Winnipeg, Canada: The University of Manitoba Centre for Higher Education Research and Development.

Kanter, R. M. (1994). Collaborative advantage: The art of alliances. Harvard Business Review, 72(4), 96-109.

Keller, G. (1999). Planning, decisions, and human nature. In M. W. Peterson, L. A. Mets, A. Trice & D. D. Dill (Eds.), ASHE reader on planning and institutional research (pp. 5-49). Needham Heights, MA: Pearson Custom Publishing.

Kezar, A. (2005). Moving from I to we: Reorganizing for collaboration in higher education. Change, 37(6), 50-57.

Knight, J. (1993). Internationalization: management strategies and issues. International Education Magazine, 6, 20-22.

Knight, J. (1994). Internationalization: Elements and checkpoints. Canadian Bureau for International Education Research, 7, 1-15.

Knight, J. (1999). Internationalisation of higher education. In J. Knight & H. de Wit (Eds.), Quality and internationalisation in higher education. Paris: Organisation for Economic Co-operation and Development.

Knight, J. (2001). Monitoring the quality and progress of Internationalization. Journal of Studies in International Education, 5(3), 228-243.

Knight, J. (2004). Internationalization remodeled: Definitions, approaches and rationales. Journal of Studies in International Education, 8(1), 5-31.

Knight, J., & de Wit, H. (1995). Strategies for internationalisation of higher education: Historical and conceptual perspectives. In H. de Wit (Ed.), Strategies for internationalisation of higher education: A comparative study of Australia, Canada, Europe, and the United States of America. Amsterdam: European Association for International Education.

Lambert, R. (1989). International studies and the undergraduate. Washington, DC: American Council on Education.

Lawler, E. E., III. (1992). The ultimate advantage: Creating the high-involvement organization. San Francisco: Jossey-Bass.

Leinwald, G. (1983). Without a nickel: The challenge of internationalizing the curriculum and the campus. Washington, DC: American Association of State Colleges and Universities.

Lerner, A. L. (1999). A strategic planning primer for higher education. Retrieved March 14, 2007, from http://www.sonoma.edu/aa/planning/Strategic_Planning_Primer.pdf

Liedtka, J. M. (1998). Linking strategic thinking with strategic planning. Strategy and Leadership, 26(4), 30-36.

Lim, G. C. (1996). Internationalization of the curriculum: Humanistic globalization approach. In C. B. Cox (Ed.), Building a world-class university: Proceedings of a campus symposium on strengthening international programs at Virginia Tech (pp. 26-50). Blacksburg: Virginia Polytechnic Institute and State University Office of International Programs.

Lim, G. C. (2003). The rationale for globalization. In G. C. Lim (Ed.), Strategy for a global university (2nd ed., pp. 3-20). East Lansing: Michigan State University.

Lionbridge. (2006). Localization industry definitions. Retrieved November 19, 2006, from http://www.lionbridge.com/kc/localization_faqs.asp

Liverpool, P. R. (1995). Positioning Virginia Tech to compete in the international arena. In P. R. Liverpool (Ed.), Building a world class university: A campus symposium on strengthening international programs at Virginia Tech.

Liverpool, P. R. (1995). Building a world class university: Positioning Virginia Tech to compete in the international arena. In C. B. Cox (Ed.), Building a world-class university: Proceedings of a campus symposium on strengthening international programs at Virginia Tech (pp. 5-18). Blacksburg, VA: Virginia Polytechnic Institute and State University Office of International Programs.

Maidstone, P. (1996). International literacy: A paradigm for change. Victoria, Canada: Centre for Curriculum, Transfer and Technology.

Mallea, J. (1977). Internationalisation of higher education and the professions. In Organisation for Economic Co-operation and Development (Ed.), International trade in professional services. Paris: Organisation for Economic Co-operation and Development.

McKellin, K. (1995). Anticipating the future: Workshops and resources for internationalizing the post-secondary campus. Vancouver, Canada: British Columbia Centre for International Education.

McKellin, K. (1998). Maintaining the momentum: The internationalization of British Columbia post secondary institutions. Victoria, Canada: British Columbia Centre for International Education.

Merkx, G. (2003). The two waves of internationalization in US higher education. International Educator, 7(1), 6-12.

Merriam, S. B. (1998). *Qualitative Research and Case Study Applications in Education.* San Francisco: Jossey-Bass, 1998.

Mestenhauser, J. A. (1998). Portraits of an international curriculum: An uncommon multidimensional perspective. In J. A. Mestenhauser & B. J. Ellingboe (Eds.), Reforming the higher education curriculum: Internationalizing the campus (pp. 3-39). Washington, DC: Oryx Press.

Mestenhauser, J. A. (2002). In search of a comprehensive approach to international education: A systems perspective. In W. Grunweig & N. Rinehart (Eds.), Rockin in Red Square: Critical approaches to international education in the age of cyberculture (pp. 165-213). New Brunswick, NJ: Transaction Publishers.

Mestenhauser, J. A., & Ellingboe, B. J. (Eds.). (1998). Reforming the higher education curriculum. Internationalizing the campus. Washington, D. C.: American Council on Education.

Miller, E. L. (1992). Internationalization of the Michigan Business School: A letter from the front. In A. M. Rugman & W. T. Stanbury (Eds.), Global Perspective: Internationalizing management education (pp. 281-300). Vancouver, Canada: University of British Columbia.

Miller, M. A. (2001). Faculty as a renewable resource. Change, 33(4), 4.

Moats-Gallagher, C. (2004). Leading the internationalization of land grant institutions: Crafting a strategic approach. Retrieved January 6, 2006, from http://www.nasulgc.org/CIP/Task%20Force/UnivLeadership.pdf

Moxon, R. W., O'Shea, E. A., Brown, M., & Escher, C. M. (2001). Changing US business needs for international expertise. In P. O'Meara, H. D. Mehlinger & R. M. A. Newman (Eds.), Changing perspectives on international education (pp. 139-157). Bloomington: Indiana University Press.

NAFSA: Association of International Educators. (2003). Internationalizing the campus 2003: Profiles of success at colleges and universities. Washington, DC: NAFSA: Association of International Educators.

NAFSA: Association of International Educators. (2004). Internationalizing the campus 2004: Profiles of success at colleges and universities. Washington, DC: NAFSA: Association of International Educators.

NAFSA: Association of International Educators. (2005). Internationalizing the campus 2005: Profiles of success at colleges and universities. Washington, DC: NAFSA: Association of International Educators.

NAFSA: Association of International Educators. (2006a). Americans call for leadership on international education: A national survey on preparation for a global society. Retrieved November 16, 2006, from http://www.nafsa.org/_/Document/_/americans_call_for_ leadership.pdf

NAFSA: Association of International Educators. (2006b). Could foreign student numbers be headed for a rebound? Retrieved November 13, 2006, from http://www.nafsa.org/press_releases.sec/press_releases.pg/06enrollsurveyrel

NAFSA: Association of International Educators. (2006c). Internationalizing the campus 2006: Profiles of success at colleges and universities. Washington, DC: NAFSA: Association of International Educators.

NAFSA: Association of International Educators. (2007). Internationalizing the campus: Selected institutions. Retrieved June 22, 2007, from http://www.nafsa.org/about.sec/leadership_recognition/senator_simon_award_for_2/internationalizing_the_6

National Association of State Universities and Land Grant Colleges. (1993). Internationalizing higher education through the faculty. Washington, DC: National Association of State Universities and Land Grant Colleges.

National Association of State Universities and Land Grant Colleges Task Force on International Education. (2004). A call to leadership: The presidential role in internationalizing the university. Retrieved September 28, 2005, from http://www.nasulgc.org/CIP/Task%20Force/ Call_to_leadership.pdf

Odgers, T., & Giroux, I. (2006, March 2-3). Internationalizing faculty: A phased approach to transforming curriculum design and instruction. Paper presented at the Internationalizing Canada's Universities, York University, Toronto, Canada.

Olson, C. L. (2005). Comprehensive internationalization: From principles to practice. Journal of Public Affairs, 8, 51-74.

Olson, C. L., Green, M. F., & Hill, B. A. (2005). Building a strategic framework for comprehensive internationalization. Washington, DC: American Council on Education.

Olson, C. L., Green, M. F., & Hill, B. A. (2006). A handbook for advancing comprehensive internationalization: What institutions can do and what students should learn. Washington, DC: American Council on Education.

Organisation for Economic Co-operation and Development. (1995). Learning beyond schooling: New forms of supply and new demands. Paris: Organisation for Economic Co-operation and Development.

Orton, J. D., & Weick, K. E. (1990). Loosely coupled systems: A reconceptualization. The Academy of Management Journal, 15(2), 203-223.

Paige, R. M. (2003). The American case: The University of Minnesota. Journal of Studies in International Education, 7(1), 52-63.

Paige, R. M. (2005). Internationalization of higher education: Performance assessment and indicators. Nagoya Journal of Higher Education, 5, 99-122.

Paige, R. M., & Mestenhauser, J. (1999). Internationalizing educational administration. Educational Administration Quarterly, 35(4), 500-517.

Parsons, C., & Fidler, B. (2005). A new theory of educational change-punctuated equilibrium: The case of the internationalization of higher education institutions. British Journal of Educational Studies, 53(4), 447-465.

Peterson, M. W. (1999). Using contextual planning to transform institutions. In M. W. Peterson, L. A. Mets, A. Trice, & D. D. Dill (Eds.), ASHE reader on planning and institutional research (pp. 60-78). Needham Heights, MA: Pearson Custom Publishing.

Piercy, N. F. (2002). Market-led, strategic change: A guide to transforming the process of going to market (3rd ed.). Oxford, UK: Butterworth-Heinemann.

Rowley, D. J., Lujan, H. D., & Dolence, M. G. (1997). Strategic change in colleges and universities: Planning to survive and prosper. San Francisco: Jossey-Bass.

Rudolph, F. (1977). Curriculum: A history of the American undergraduate course of study since 1636. San Francisco: Jossey-Bass.

Schoorman, D. (1999). The pedagogical implications of diverse conceptualizations of internationalization: A US-based case study. Journal of Studies in International Education, 3(2), 19-46.

Scott, R. A. (1992). Campus developments in response to the challenges of internationalization: The case of Ramapo College of New Jersey. Springfield, VA: CBIS Federal.

Shute, J. (2002). The influence of faculty in shaping internationalization. In S. Bond & C. Bowry (Eds.), Connections and complexities: The internationalization of higher education in Canada (pp. 114-123). Winnipeg, Canada: University of Manitoba Centre for Higher Education Research and Development.

Siaya, L., & Hayward, F. (2001). Public experience, attitudes, and knowledge: A report on two national surveys about international education. Washington, DC: American Council on Education.

Siaya, L., & Hayward, F. (2003). Mapping internationalization on US campuses: Final report. Washington, DC: American Council on Education.

Smuckler, R. H. (2003). A university turns to the world. East Lansing, MI: Michigan State University Press.

Steers, R. M., & Ungsen, G. R. (1992). In search of the holy grail: Reflections on the internationalization of business education. In A. M. Rugman & W. T. Stanbury (Eds.), Global perspective: Internationalizing management education (pp. 301-316). Vancouver, Canada: University of British Columbia.

Sun Developer Network. (2006). Java internationalization. Retrieved November 19, 2006, from http://java.sun.com/javase/technologies/core/basic/intl/

Thullen, M., Heyl, J. D., & Brownell, B. (2002). The chief international education administrator (CIEA) as an agent for organisational change (No. EAIE Occasional Paper 14). Amsterdam, the Netherlands: European Association for International Education.

Tonkin, H., & Edwards, J. (1981). The world in the curriculum. New Rochelle, NY: Change Magazine Press.

Venn, J. (1880). On the diagrammatic and mechanical representation of propositions and reasonings. The London Edinburgh and Dublin Philosophical Magazine and Journal of Science, 9, 1-18.

Viers, C. J. (1998). Internationalization of American higher education: A review of the literature. International Review, 8(1), 27-46.

Viers, C. J. (2003). Faculty engaged in international scholarship: A study of when, how, and why. Dissertation Abstracts International, 64(12), 4389A. (UMI No. 3116059).

Weick, K. E. (1976). Educational organizations as loosely coupled systems. Administrative Science Quarterly, 21(1), 1-19.

Weick, K. E. (1982). Management of organizational change among loosely coupled elements. In P. S. Goodman (Ed.), Change in organizations (pp. 375-408). San Francisco: Jossey-Bass.

Welsh, A. R. (1997). The peripatetic professor: The internationalization of the academic profession. Higher Education, 34(3), 323-245.

Whalley, T. (1997). Best practices for internationalizing the curriculum. Victoria, Canada: Ministry of Education, Skills, and Training and the Centre for Curriculum, Transfer and Technology.

Wood, R. J. (1990). Toward cultural empathy: A framework for global education. Educational Record, 71(4), 9-13.

Index

A

C

D

E

F

I

OMPLICATED

A BOOK SERIES OF CURRICULUM STUDIES

This series employs research completed in various disciplines to construct textbooks that will enable public school teachers to reoccupy a vacated public domain—not simply as "consumers" of knowledge, but as active participants in a "complicated conversation" that they themselves will lead. In drawing promiscuously but critically from various academic disciplines and from popular culture, this series will attempt to create a conceptual montage for the teacher who understands that positionality as aspiring to reconstruct a "public" space. *Complicated Conversation* works to resuscitate the progressive project—an educational project in which self-realization and democratization are inevitably intertwined; its task as the new century begins is nothing less than the intellectual formation of a public sphere in education.

The series editor is:

Dr. William F. Pinar
Department of Curriculum Studies
2125 Main Mall
Faculty of Education
University of British Columbia
Vancouver, British Columbia V6T 1Z4
CANADA

To order other books in this series, please contact our Customer Service Department:

(800) 770-LANG (within the U.S.)
(212) 647-7706 (outside the U.S.)
(212) 647-7707 FAX

Or browse online by series:

www.peterlang.com